HOW SHOULD I LOVE YOU?

How Should I Love You?

DWIGHT HERVEY SMALL

1817

Published in San Francisco by Harper & Row, Publishers

NEW YORK, HAGERSTOWN, SAN FRANCISCO, LONDON

FIRST EDITION

Designed by Jim Mennick

Library of Congress Cataloging in Publication Data

Small, Dwight Hervey.
  HOW SHOULD I LOVE YOU?

  Includes bibliographical references.
  1. Love (Theology) 2. Love. I. Title.
BV4639.S62   1979   248'.4   78-20588
ISBN 0-06-067398-2

---

79 80 81 82 83 10 9 8 7 6 5 4 3 2 1

To Lynne and Jim,
Shay and Karl

Contents

Abbreviations

Scripture references are from the Revised Standard Version, unless otherwise indicated by the following abbreviations:

King James Version	KJV
The Living Bible	TLB
New American Standard Bible	NASB
The New Testament in Modern English by J. B. Phillips	JBP

Acknowledgments

IN THE evolution of this book the author is indebted to individuals beyond the possibility of recall. Colleagues at Westmont College, students in the twenty semesters during which *Contemporary Christian Marriage* has been taught, professionals in the college counselling center of which the author has been a staff member for ten years, countless persons younger and older alike who have attended Marriage Seminars or youth conferences across the country for twenty-five years, and not least Ned Divelbiss of the Library staff of the college who aided in the research. And since every manuscript has its deficiencies, the special people at Harper & Row are here recognized for major facilitation in bringing about largescale revisions: the demanding standards of my editor Roy M. Carlisle, and the efficient handling of detail and scheduling by Kathy Reigstad. Susan Weisberg served as a copyeditor par excellence, working as a capable critic whose insights brought about that healthy tension out of which alterations of some magnitude were made. Finally, to my wife, Ruth, goes profound thanks for her continuing reinforcement through the sacrifices occasioned by a writing career which must be sandwiched into a teaching career, and all too often absorbing whole weekends and vacation periods.

Introduction

A POPULAR song of a few years back, still a favorite with many audiences, asks, "What is this thing called love?" Can we ever hope to understand the true and intricate nature of love? Or, as some well-credentialed skeptics have suggested, is "love" just an illusion that tantalizes and deceives its innocent devotees? Poets, novelists, song writers, philosophers, theologians, and psychologists, too—all have taken their turn. The literature is voluminous, the theories myriad. Can we really know what love is?

The question recalls the story of the little fellow who was engaged in finger painting. What a glorious mess it was! He happened to have learned it at Sunday school, so there was some relevance to his answer when his mother asked what he was drawing. The child answered, "This is a picture of God." Mother, not wanting her son to start life as a theological heretic, replied, "But, dear, no one knows what God looks like." Unabashed, the youngster responded without hesitation, "They will when I get done."

Perhaps it's too much to expect that those who "get done" with this book will know what love is in all of its meanings and nuances. Hopefully, however, they should know considerably more than before they started, simply because the analysis presented here is distilled from a vast literature, much of which is not readily available to the average reader. Hopefully, too, what I've taught for years in college courses and given in marriage seminars across the nation will be helpful to a larger audience in its published form.

This book is somewhat unique in both the scope and the method of its examination of love. Taking a panoramic view, it begins with the modes and myths of romantic love, going from there to the miracle of caring love. It seeks to integrate concepts of love, both human and divine, from *eros* to *agape*. The book is unique also in its scope of application—to young people and working singles and to marrieds with a wealth of experience behind them. The psychology of loving is blended together with a Christian philosophy of love's relation to life—life's joys and successes, life's pains and disappointments. Because love is experienced in its deviations and illusions, what we presently know about infatuation, romantic myths, and pseudo-loves based on ego-needs all will come into the range of our consideration in the following chapters.

Romantic love is a tricky business. It is also big business, judging from the prominence given it by the media and the dramatic arts. In American life it is virtually cultic; we all but do obeisance to it. Of course, we deny its trickery. Nonetheless, though we minimize its dominant role in courtship, we never fail to lament its loss in marriage. We profess to marry for love yet turn to people other than our spouses for the "real thing." There seems nothing we are more ambivalent about than romantic love, and nothing with greater power to deceive husbands or wives who question the changing nature of married love and who cast glances at attractive individuals waiting in the wings, ready to prove what love can really be like.

With romantic love as the foil—the better to draw sharp contrasts—we move on to the characteristics of mature, caring love. Here is love for a truly intimate partnership, love with the kind of inherent strength and integrity to give it staying power. The spontaneous, exciting, and dramatic features of romantic love, as well as the more stable, predictable, and deeper dimensions of caring love are all aspects we need to grasp intelligently to avoid the traps and the disillusionments that await the innocent and naive.

The New Testament presents a theology of love suited to our deepest needs and profoundest satisfactions. Human love is redeemable; this is one of the major themes of Scripture. Once God's love in Christ is experienced for ourselves, there is no reason ever to fear the demise of romantic love or to lament its power to elude our fondest expectations. There is a better way.

For those who prefer the whole story, who are curious enough to enjoy probing origins and historical expressions, the two initial chapters of this book are a foundation for what follows. The first chapter concerns the rise of romantic love in history, especially how it developed into its contemporary form in the United States, from here to be exported throughout the Western world via our film industry. The second chapter traces the dynamics of romantic love as portrayed in the novels of a particularly significant place and period, a time when romantic love was coming into its own. Romantic literature, particularly that of France, has influenced every generation up to and including our own.

For those whose interest lies more narrowly in the psychology of loving, the first two chapters may be either skimmed or skipped. But just this word: however little you may be interested in history or literature, even brief exposure can greatly enlarge your grasp of what follows. So I encourage the effort; the story is an intriguing one!

The final section of the book has its own distinctiveness. Having climbed to the heights of what it means to care for another person in love's deepest commitment, we take a look at how love can resolve conflicts and heal brokenness in the daily lives of husbands and wives. We want to know how love can make the difference when the going is tough or just humdrum. Techniques and illustrations will help bring it all together. Along with some prods to self-examination, there should be ample indication of how to implement one's new understanding with a transformed lifestyle—or should we say "lovestyle"?

PART I

Romantic Love:
Its Modes and Myths

~ 1

Whoever Tilted Love Toward Romance?

Love is the tyrant of the heart; it darkens
Reason, confounds discretions; deaf to counsel,
It runs a headlong course to desperate madness.

JOHN FORD, *The Lover's Melancholy*

*P*ERHAPS you've come to feel like the little girl whose father was trying to explain why he would no longer be living with her and her mother, because they were getting a divorce. He says he still wants to be her father but not her mother's husband. "I still love you," he says, "but I no longer love your mother." It's all too confusing for the little girl, and finally she says, "I'm getting sick of big words like love."

The Many Faces of Love

Love is many things to many people in many societies in many different times. In tennis love means nothing, whereas in marriage it means everything. In the rest of life it can mean most anything at all. Love is a feeling, yet love is also a commitment. Love has to do with sentiment, yet it must transcend sentiment. Love is necessary to human life and its full development, yet love is something we learn or do not learn. Furthermore, as we learn loving in our earliest relations with other people, so we learn nonloving as well. Only too soon we discover that human love can be conditional when it shouldn't be and not reliable when it should be. How complex and disconcerting human love can be!

There is familial love, the love between parents and children—the first love most of us experience in life. Then there is peer love, romantic love, sexual love, and ultimately the stable, enduring love of devoted couples in marriage. Besides human love there is divine love, a unique expression of God's love from which human beings can derive a higher love with self-transcending qualities. The ancient Greeks were perhaps among the first to distinguish the major forms of love, employing three words principally to bring this out. Of these three words, the New Testament singled out one—*agape*—and invested it with the superlative meanings encompassing the New Testament teaching about the unconditional, redemptive love of God for humanity—a love that we may assimilate into our own being, expressing it to one another. Yes, love has many faces.

Our initial quest is to understand the two distinct forms of love that characterize heterosexual relationships—the *romantic* and the *marital*. What qualities make each of these forms distinct? How do the two forms relate? How do they differ? Does love progress from one to the other? Does genuine love incorporate something of both forms? What are the popular myths that surround romantic love? What psychodynamics can we identify? Are there pitfalls to recognize and avoid? Why are young people especially prone to romantic allurements? And why is the romantic affair such an extraordinary threat in the middle years of marriage? We will begin with the pseudo-loves so pervasive in our culture and then move on to the genuine loves that ennoble and enrich life.

A New Love for a New World

To understand romantic sentiment and passion, we must view it as a rather recent phenomenon in the history and culture of the Western world. However, romantic love, as the American philosopher William James pointed out some years ago, is no new development in the human repertoire; it is new only in the sense that it is now developed in mass culture. Though romantic love has been present for a long time, particular societies in particular eras have elevated it to a highly prized value. Contemporary theologian Suzanne Lilar discovers the amorous emotion as far back as the time of Homer, and she goes so far as to say that passionate love is among the "primitive data of the human condition."[1] The social historian Robert Briffault traced narratives expressing passionate love in ancient Celtic literature.[2] So romantic love has been with us for a long time in one form or another.

Underlying our present culture of love are clear historical roots, revealing why romantic love is both the strength and the weakness of American marriage. In retrospect we see that the manners of past times commonly reflect themselves in the literature of the times, and in turn the literature helps shape the manners of its period. It is not surprising, then, that French romantic novels from the seventeenth century on reflected the times in which the novelists lived—times quite different from those preceding but times that were to leave an indelible imprint on the future of Western civilization.

The greatest of the romantic eras are few in number. What began in a small way in the twelfth century, only to be short-lived, was resumed in the seventeenth century, although, to be sure, in an entirely different social setting. The development we trace to the seventeenth century in France has been refined and imported into the culture of our own day. It is thus that we see an evolution of romantic sentiment and the psychodynamics that now prevail in heterosexual relationships in most of the societies of the Western world.

For most of the centuries prior to the modern era romantic love between men and women simply didn't exist as a major social phenomenon. At certain periods and in certain highly developed societies it flourished for a time, but this was the extraordinary; historical and cultural conditions were heavily weighted against it. Understandably, romantic pursuits are a luxury not possible among people who necessarily must focus all their energies on the day-to-day exigencies just to ensure a minimal subsistence. Psychologist Vernon Grant observes that a society must mature socially and economically before it can release some of its members for what amounts to emotional recreation. It is a leisured people that can develop the more complex forms of play, and romantic involvement is definitely a type of play; an intriguing game, no less!

Two Basic Loves

What we mean by the kind of love that binds a man and woman together isn't easy to determine. To ask the question is not to come up with answers so much as to come up with additional questions. Like most other things, love has its causes, its characteristics, and its consequences. But the problem is simply that there are two basic forms of love between men and women: the *romantic*, which lies outside of and usually prior to marriage, and the *affiliative*, which is the love bond of an enduring relationship such as marriage. If we distinguish clearly between the two, discovering how they logically and naturally follow one after the other, then our definitions of love are not quite so difficult to come by after all.

It is fascinating to observe that heterosexual love ranges from the possibility of being madly in love with a total stranger, about whom one may know nothing whatever, not even a name, to a most enduring commitment, an intimate life partnership. Love may range from being merely a fantasized idealization, an ego-trip (*"You* make *me* love *me* more"), an emotional dependency heavily laden with irrational passions, to its near opposite—a realistic, caring companionship, more rational, less passionate, yet deeply satisfying. Love, it seems, may come upon a person as a dramatic, unpredictable encounter, with all the elements of surprise and spontaneous impact, or it may grow in the form of a close, secure, rewarding relationship between two total personalities; less exciting and more predictable, to be sure, and yet also more stable and enduring.

Unless our two categories are kept distinct, how easily we can confuse genuine love with other things, such as infatuation, sexual desire, the satisfaction of emotional hungers, or a desire for social status. Love may be confused with the diminishing of loneliness or social isolation, even with lessening the pain of alienation. There is even the possibility that what passes for love is merely one person's satisfaction from wielding emotional power over another.

At best, romantic love is a prelude to a genuine, caring love; an initial step, as it were. But today's television soaps and newsstand slicks subtly condition us to believe that romantic love is a must experience if we are not to be deprived of one of life's greatest benefits. All the while the myth persists among the young that romantic love is a mystic force beyond all power of rational analysis. If this is true, it follows that romantic love is beyond control, too. At the same time, we have nurtured a pseudo-sophistication that denies the prevalence of irrational, myth-laden romance in our supposedly more psychologically aware society. Despite this anomaly the romantic mode is with us still. Our avant-garde friends may regard romantic love as a "peak" experience, to use the late psychologist Abraham Maslow's term, or a "high." However, it is far more complex and pervasive than this.

The Development of Romantic Love

The ancients didn't make the passions of love the central theme of their fiction. Among the Romans, Vergil and others had some vision of the torments of the love we call romantic, but only Ovid captured these emotions.

In 2 B.C., when Ovid was forty-one, he wrote his long instructional poem *Ars Amatoria—The Art of Love*—which was the first textbook, we might say, on methods of flirting, attracting lovers, seducing the desired individual, and consummating adultery. It was largely about seduction and sexual infidelity, with eloquent detail. Ovid patterned it after philosophical and educational treatises, calling himself the "tutor" of the art of love. Romans generally agreed and said that Ovid had educated an entire generation in the techniques of love. His work was revered as a detailed guidebook for playing an elegant game. It is the game that recalls students of romantic love to this master of antiquity.

Emperor Augustus banished his granddaughter Julia for the same reason he had exiled his daughter, also named Julia—for adultery. Among the granddaughter's friends was Ovid, who in time was also banished, apparently because he was in some way linked with the disgrace of the younger Julia. He had been popular in the highest circles, a position made possible by his inherited wealth, his amiable manners and wit. He devoted his life to literature and the pursuit of amorous amusement. His wives apparently interested him little; instead, he was intrigued by the women he wooed and won for pure sport. As he wrote in his earliest poems, the *Amores*, "there are a hundred causes to keep me always in love."

According to Ovid, the nature of love was conquest, and the art of seduction was cultivated in terms of hunting for quarry.[3] Among the sophisticated devices that made up his instructions was writing flattering and earnest love letters, intense though covert looking, subtle gestures, touching feet under the table, going to pains to do pleasing errands, complimenting generously, wearing spotless well-fitting clothes, and in general appearing an impeccable person.

Ovid can be considered the only great love poet before Dante, who, in the Middle Ages, idealized his love for Beatrice, whom he worshipped from afar. In the classic period of the Greeks Plato stood out as the one who had much to say about love in its many forms. When we use the term *platonic love,* we go back to Plato. Eros was the god of passionate love, and from this Greek name we derive, quite appropriately, our word *erotic,* a term that stands for the sensual, passionate love of men and women. When love went beyond simple desire, it was regarded by the Greeks as simply love madness. For this they also had a term—*eromania*—the madness of erotic love. Eromania held individuals in its spell to the point of affecting their very behavior. Only unruly passions could come of such enchantment, such madness.

It isn't until the twelfth century that a culture of romantic love emerged in the so-called courts of love and in the accompanying chivalric romances written at that time. Not until that period do we approach the complex sentiments that Blaise Pascal later discussed under the title *The Passions of Love.*

Romantic involvement owes much of its rise to the changing status of women and the new social roles that can be traced back to the first century. Christianity had given women an altogether different status than they had enjoyed hitherto. At the same time in Greece a class of women were held in especially high regard—the educated, socially emancipated *hetairae,* with whom aristrocratic men had a very special relationship. These women were companionate, good conversationalists, and provided a cultural relationship that wives were untrained to provide. The *hetairae* were also trained in the art of love making and provided casual, unencumbered sexual liaisons that were not regarded as in any way threatening to marriage. These women attained a social stature of their own so that to love them meant to appreciate them as individuals. To court their favor meant at least a minimal understanding of what it took to attract their interest and affection. Romantic interaction was at least visible as a social dynamic.

It was Christianity that placed upon both men and women the new constraints of modesty, teaching Christian men in particular that there were moral obstacles inhibiting the long-standing, unquestioned prerogatives with women that men had assumed for themselves so freely. Interestingly, this new morality served to intensify the desires women were able to arouse, desires enhanced by women's lesser accessability. Relationships must now be more personal, too, relating to the worth of every person as an individual loved by God. For women shared in the redemption through Christ just as men did. Thus was begun a new direction in the love relations of men and women. Had the concepts of Christian personal morality prevailed in the following centuries, we might have seen a magnificent development of love. Unfortunately, the loss of Christian doctrine that occurred so soon and that lasted throughout the thousand years we know as the Dark Ages seemed to cancel any gains the new faith promised. It was to be centuries before the status of women would, in fact, be elevated to the vision of the New Testament. As truth was distorted, so life was warped and left in an undeveloped stage. Love itself suffered an eclipse.

Early in Christianity the Virgin Mary was exalted as a pristine model for womanhood, idealized in her supposed perfections into something more than human. As Jesus' mother, she was worshipped almost as though she were a member of the Godhead. However, she came to represent not only the mother of God but also the epitome of perfect womanhood placed on an inaccessible pedestal. From the fifth century on the adoration of Mary increased in ardor, multiplying fantasies of feminine perfection and mystique. Here was the mystical adoration of a divine human being, idealized in theology. Before long her perfections had been established in the popular imagination, an idealization all the more possible since she was not a living person inhabiting the real world of men and women. In all likelihood the dreary circumstances of life in those times required the invention of such a figure in popular imagination, and Mary was the likely one to fill this need. Celibate priests were among her secret lovers. Adoration expressed in the religious poetry of, for example Bernard of Clairvaux, is in part romantic and in some places clearly erotic.

It could be expected that the adoration directed to the Virgin Mary would, at some favorable time, be extended to include certain contemporary members of the female sex, at least its courtly representatives. It was only a matter of time before the connection between Mary and women generally would be made. She was the *feminine principle*—tender, compassionate, full of love and kindness, self-sacrificing, and nurturant. The actual transposition of perfections was to come about in the Middle Ages. The roles relating to female perfection were to be acted out by knights and ladies, poets and troubadours. It was the Age of Chivalry. Love was to take on the character of adoration.

The romantic tales soon to sweep Europe developed about the time of the Crusades for at least two discernible reasons. They appealed to crusading pilgrims who spent long, lonely months away from home and family. These pilgrims were very numerous at the time when every man, it seemed, yearned to go to Jerusalem. Deprived of the society of women, they took pleasure in hearing the tales whose unreal heroines were romantic personages about whom they could fantasize to their heart's desire. These tales combined the heroic and the romantic.

A second group to whom the romances appealed was that class of privileged women who occupied an eminent place in society. They longed for men to be like Lancelot in the stories of the Round Table or like Tristan in his devotion to Isolde. Such women envisioned themselves not only as the desired among women but as the courted as well, vicariously living out these exciting tales. So it was that the romances of chivalry were powerful elements of popular aspiration.

Courtly Love

During so many centuries, when marriages were arranged by families for reasons of economic, social, or even political convenience, heterosexual love with fierce emotional passion was a thing unknown. It occurred, of course, but only as a furtive, little-recognized personal experience of the few. Conjugal contracts were not born of rapturous fantasies or passions. Thus any romantic notions of love could only take on an idealized form, woven for the most part into the fabric of chivalry and courtly manners. Knights adored their ladies of the court not their wives. They performed feats of courage in the name of the idolized lady they could never touch and whose favors were given from afar. In more decadent days this led to the adulterous adventures that were the sport of the leisured aristocracy. Southern France was the area where this style was first centered, and France thus was the nation where romantic love was to reappear several centuries later.

Troubadours sang of daring deeds done for love, beguiling lonely ladies of the court who had little to do but wait for their lords to return from the crusades. These ladies could hardly get excited anticipating the return of some crusty old lord, worn and aging, smelling of his horse and acting out the coarseness of months of uncultured life with battle-lusting comrades. The young squires of the court casting burning glances of adoration at her from the courtyard brought a flush to a lady's cheek and exciting fantasies to her imagination. Many a window was left unbarred at night, and many a young squire, encouraged by little tokens of his lady's favor, proved his devotion and ardor—his reckless abandon in the name of love—by boldly scaling the castle walls to his lady's chamber.

In truth, knight-errantry was less inspired by a desire to benefit women or to bring them supreme pleasure than by personal ambition to gratify masculine vanity. Gail Fullerton, President of San Jose State University, writes of this aberration.[4] Knights rode about the countryside in quest of adventure, ostensibly in the service of an adored lady, but more probably in need of an outlet for their brutish energies pent up in times of peace. Cervantes made fun of this chivalry and its contorted romantic theme as he depicted Don Quixote jousting windmills for his Dulcinea, in whose honor and for whose love he braved the imaginary foe. Each knight had his own Dulcinea, for whose love and favor he engaged in all sorts of combats. Every knight he encountered was a challenge to acknowledge that *his* Dulcinea was indeed the most beautiful lady in all the world. Of course, the other knight echoed the challenge in behalf of *his* Dulcinea, and the chivalrous duel was set. Supposedly, the victor was living proof of the superior beauty and honor of his lady. Little matter that perhaps neither knight had ever so much as been close to the lady under whose banner he fought. All this, of course, was quite absurd, but it fulfilled a need for romantic passions to express themselves. It served as a means of self-affirmation, and it demonstrated how much romantic passion exists as a condition within an individual's own imagination. The psychology of it all is stimulated more by one's inner need than by the actual object of his amorous sentiments.

The most famous love affair of the Middle Ages was that of Abélard and Héloïse, who lived during the eleventh and twelfth centuries, when courtly love flourished.

Abélard was a theologian and philosopher. By the year 1118, when he was thirty-eight years old, he had attracted students from every corner of Europe. Although chaste until then, he thought it time to experience the earthly solaces. He heard of an eighteen-year-old girl in Paris, Héloïse, niece of the Canon Fulbert. Despite her youth, she was already well versed in Latin, Greek, and Hebrew, and was regarded as not only brilliant but lovely to look at. Abélard decided to "join her with myself in love," so he contrived to become a lodger at Fulbert's home. Fulbert, delighted to have a renowned scholar residing with him, not only welcomed Abélard but played into his hands by suggesting that he might instruct Héloïse at any hour.

Disturbed by the persistent rumors of an affair between the two, Fulbert eventually sent Abélard away, but Héloïse was already pregnant. One night, in Fulbert's absence, Abélard and Héloïse eloped and fled to Abélard's home in Brittany, out of Fulbert's jurisdiction. However, with time to think about his future in the church, Abélard desired peace with Fulbert. He returned to Paris to propose marriage with Héloïse, on the condition that the marriage be by secret vow. Thus, Abélard reasoned, he could continue his career without fear of discovery.

Contrary to his promise, Fulbert leaked the news. Héloïse, to protect Abélard, swore that she was not his wife but only his mistress. At Abélard's urging, Héloïse fled to the Argenteuil convent near Paris and became a nun. There she and Abélard were able to meet secretly on occasion. Fulbert, meanwhile, thought Abélard had become tired of Héloïse, and assumed that this was her reason for becoming a nun. Unable to stand idly by while thinking that Abélard had degraded Héloïse, he bribed Abélard's servant, and as Abélard slept a band of men sprang upon him and castrated him. The disconsolate Abélard ordered Héloïse to take the nun's veil, for until now she had not taken vows. His intent was to follow and become a monk.

Much of what we know of the lovers is based on an exchange of letters—three by her, four by him, and one by him to an unnamed friend that somehow passed through her hands. Interestingly, the letters were written some years after Abélard's castration. The first two of hers made Héloïse a most admired woman in history. She became the image of the unusually selfless woman, willing to do anything for her lover. Here is the love of absolute surrender and self-abnegation. No qualifications, no moral concerns, no guilt feelings—only full compliance with Abélard's wishes. Héloïse is the model of a woman who is both beautiful and educated and also sensuous and vibrant—a woman who enjoyed the romantic and erotic dimensions of love. She is thus a heroic woman, the embodiment of a compelling, romantic love ideal. Thus was the woman's role in romantic love turned into what became an enduring stereotype.

In the development of courtly love women who held the status of nobility became highly regarded as ideal beings. Their favors might be won by masculine vitality and brave sacrifice. The courtly lover, in consequence of his demonstrated valor in the name of his lady, derived virtue and status for himself. He took on the much-desired qualities from the object of his adoration and service. The lady became an extension of himself—his wished-for self, as it were. His mighty passion of love spoke of honor, courage, sacrifice of self, contempt for worldly goods and even life itself. Such adoring love was equated with a spiritual felicity, meriting for its possessor a surpassing beatitude. Such was the mystique of love. In this way a man could identify with something more ideal and worthy than himself. The mystical union contributed nobility and worth to him when otherwise he could see little of these wished-for qualities in himself alone.

If, in this way, womanhood was perfected through natural feminine weakness combined with feminine beauty, so manhood was perfected through adoring, protecting, and serving a woman. Womanhood, represented by the lady he adored and served, was the true cause of a man's tender passions and gentle manners. For his part he learned the nobility of unselfish aspirations, the tempering of his rudeness. Women, unused to such devotion, learned to become as extravagantly coy as men were gallant. So the game of romantic liaisons was born in the culture of the Age of Chivalry. It was a time and place for games of love.

Absurd? Yes. Functional? Yes, very much so. To the dull and strictly utilitarian relations between men and women, an imaginative dimension had been added. Life had a new hue. Love was now supersensual, transcending sheer sexual lust. Relationships now had a highly personal quality never before achieved. So it can be granted that courtly love, despite its excesses and illusions, did idealize and refine sexual expression, linking it to devotion, personal feelings of desire, gentleness necessary to the winning of another's heart, and the giving of oneself to another.

For men and women to engage in romantic attachments, they must have sufficient leisure to daydream and fantasize, leisure to play the game called love. Outside the courts and salons of a leisured society, the aristocracy of former days, this was not possible. The life of common men and women alike was one of unrelenting labor just to subsist. Life was not a game; the hard realities precluded anything that would suggest a romantic view of things.

In fact, the romantic era built upon courtly love was brief and involved a relatively small segment of the population. This period was followed by a long epoch of social disorder and violence—the time of the Hundred Years' War and the religious wars. Courtly love was largely eclipsed by the demand of warfare for the energies of all the people. Then finally, at the beginning of the seventeenth century, in the wake of more peaceful and prosperous times, leisure, social games, and the sentiments of love reappeared. As soon as the rising middle class in Europe could emulate the aristocracy, romantic love was widely pursued by the common people, especially in the burgeoning cities. Eventually a growing tradition made romantic love the prelude to marriage, but this was long in coming.

Love became an emotion inspired by the one-and-only. An axiomatic part of the romantic tradition was that one truly loved but once. Recognizing the individuality of the beloved gave a particularly supreme quality to the experience of love, making it unthinkable that any other than the beloved could inspire the same emotion. As in the days of chivalry, *to be loved* was honorable (for it implied supreme worth), and *to love* was glorious (as it pledged the lover to the ultimate sacrifice of the self). All the essential components of romantic love are seen emerging at this point in history. Ironically, a large part of courtly behavior developed to mock both religion and the prevailing system of marriage. Inasmuch as marriage was a duty more than a pleasure, romantic love can be seen as a countermeasure. However, the countermeasure was to prevail and eventually influence marriage itself. We shall note the early indications of this during the Renaissance period.

A summary of the development of ideas of love through the ages is provided by Bernard Murstein. "The twelfth century saw the flourishing of 'courtly love,' a phenomenon whose importance is intensely debated by contemporary medievalists. To some it was a prototype, a precursor of the romanticism that penetrated the relationship between the sexes in the nineteenth and twentieth centuries. To others it was a minor art form, never predominant even in the twelfth century, but inflated in importance by the nineteenth century writer, Gaston Paris, who coined the term 'courtly love.' "[5]

Courtly love, according to Murstein, "embodied the relationship between aspiring lovers and their noble ladies. Its principal exponents, lyric poets or poet-musicians—*troubadours*—composed poems and songs expressing a code whose chief tenets were the ennobling power of love; the conception of love as a burning, rarely extinguished passion; the impossibility of love between husband and wife; the elevation of the beloved to a position superior to that of the suppliant, and the idea of fidelity between lovers (at least while they were in love)."[6]

Thus romantic love and marriage were two separate entities that fulfilled entirely separate needs. So long as the lovers remained sexually "virtuous," the husband's marital rights were safeguarded and the rules of chivalry upheld. As knighthood declined, however, so did the sexual inhibitions of the knights and ladies, and in the court society of the Baroque and Rococo periods the brave deeds of gallants were rewarded with sexual favors. So began the fusion of sex and love; and perhaps, too, began the confusion of sex with love.

The Comtesse de Champagne told her court in 1174, "Love cannot extend its rights over two married persons." One could not love someone who could not be longed for—for instance, one's wife. If one were to marry one's love, one would exchange the sweet torment of desire, the yearning, for that which fulfills it. Thus the tension of hope would be replaced by the comfort of certainty. In the past people seldom thought of joining marriage to love. Each state had its own motive power; one primed for a lifelong journey, the other for an ardent improvisation, a voyage of discovery. The spontaneous passion of love stands in contrast to the deliberate permanence of marriage.

"The "ennobling power of love" refers to the process of loving rather than to the beloved. The famous troubadour Bernard de Ventadour said, "By nothing is man made so worthy as by love and the courting of women, for thence arise delight and song and all that pertains to excellence."[7]

The Albigensian Crusade (1209–1218), together with the dreaded Inquisition, brought the massacre of thousands in southern France. Murstein writes: "The Albigensian Crusade resulted in an inhibition of sensual expression in troubadourian poetry and in a bowdlerizing of the content of the poems. The lady of the troubadour was no longer a woman of the flesh; she became either the Virgin Mary (Madonna) or a heavenly surrogate. To love women as sexual objects was wrong; to love the spark of God in them was good."[8] As Denis de Rougemont puts it, there was now "in short, lyricism, eroticism, and mysticism unleashed over all of Europe, and speaking one and the same language."[9]

Adoring Love—Dante Alighieri

As we proceed to analyze romantic love, we shall see it as a form of adoration. Adoration is the perception and worship of something beyond oneself. One suddenly feels a new quality of life. A change is brought about in one's inner being, a new state of mind. The impression of the object of adoration intensifies as though one's eyes had a new power to reveal a wholly different aspect of the world. There is a bouyancy as one is introduced to a hitherto unknown domain, surpassing all previous visions. It is a lyrical state, in which the image of the person adored remains constantly present as vivid reality. All other preoccupations vanish before this singular obsession. The image of the beloved is central to all perception. While thinking that one loves the other, in reality one loves the subjective state that the image of the other arouses.

Psychoanalyst Hubert Benoit, in discussing adoration as a psychic phenomenon, writes, "To a lover of great imaginative power, the real woman is hardly necessary."[10] In adoration, he says, one has projected something upon the other that can thenceforth be enjoyed only through that person.

During the Middle Ages, as we've noted, ladies were adored for years without knowing it. Adoring lovers were content to love without desiring so much as a kiss. The most famous and influential example is Dante Alighieri's celebrated love for Beatrice. The account and its significance is intriguing.

In the *Vita Nuova* Danta tells us how he first saw Beatrice in the year 1274, when he was only nine years old and she was slightly younger. Immediately he began to worship her with a pure and inspiring love. He never spoke one word to her, however, and scarcely hoped to. No efforts were made to meet her, and he saw her only at rare intervals. In fact, it was nine years before they met a second time, when Dante was eighteen. Then a simple salutation from Beatrice caused him to tremble with passion. But Beatrice, irked by what she perceived as his negligence, subsequently refused his salutation. Deeply pained, Dante sought to express his love in disinterested praise. Beatrice married soon thereafter, and died while still in her twenties. Her death impressed Dante that to concentrate upon a beloved's physical existence was only to experience grief and powerlessness. The awesome power of the *donna* came, as he reasoned, from the spirit of God that shone through her earthly form.

A brilliant analysis of Dante's experience is found in the *The Figure of Beatrice: A Study in Dante* by Charles Williams, Oxford mentor of T.S. Eliot, C.S. Lewis, and Dorothy Sayers.[11] Williams chose Dante and Beatrice as his principal image of romantic love. Because Dante was not only a romantic lover but also one of the greatest of poets, he reported his reactions in language of surpassing precision, clarity, and beauty. Further, as Mary McDermott Shideler[12] observes, the historical events comprise almost the irreducible minimum for romantic love: Dante never became involved in the complications intrinsic to close friendship with his beloved, not to mention those of courtship or marriage. The facts of falling in love and of being in love stand here with elemental simplicity.

Dante's significance for a theology of romantic love, says Shideler, lies in his explicit awareness of Beatrice as an image and in the penetration with which he described himself (the imagist and lover), Beatrice (the image and beloved), and the structure of the relationship between them.

Williams points to one characteristic that unites all events properly termed romantic—*the shock of an intense personal experience.* Something is suddenly and shatteringly discovered, involving the whole of one's being in a total response. Dante described it as an "astonishment of the mind." [13] In Shideler's words, it is essentially a moment—brief or prolonged—of violent change, after which nothing will ever be the same again. And it has two salient features: givenness and passion. [14] To say that the romantic shock is "given" means simply that it is a gift, something bestowed upon the romantic by forces beyond his or her control. Dante did not decide to fall in love with Beatrice; such a moment can be desired but not willed. Some other kinds of love are subject to our will, as we shall see later on, but the romantic is not.

"The romantic moment produces a conversion in the lover's world view: he turns away from a former orientation, and toward something new which is usually an extreme either of order and delight or of chaos and horror. A new being inhabits a new world of ecstasy and beauty. The lover moves for a time in a universe which is strange to him, and where he is strange to himself." [15]

Williams summarizes Dante's experience in a way that captures the romantic moment:

Dante is, it seems, "satisfied" by Beatrice; his sensations, his emotions, his ideas, his faith, coalesce. Perfection in some strange sense exists, and walks down the street of Florence to meet him. She is "the youngest of the Angels"; her image in his thought "is an exultation of Love to subdue him," yet so perfect that Love never acts without "the faithful counsel of reason, wherever such counsel was useful to be heard"; she is "the destroyer of all evil and the queen of all good"; she is the equivalent of heaven itself. . . . He says that when she met him in the street and said good-morning, he was so highly moved that he was, for the moment, in a state of complete good-will, complete *caritas* toward everyone. If anyone had at that moment done him an injury, he would necessarily have forgiven him. He has not only fallen in love; he is, strictly, "in love." He is aware of that beyond everything; "if anyone had asked me a question I should have been able to answer only 'Love.' ".... "I have been," he said soon after that description, "at that point of life beyond which he who passes cannot return"; and this indeed is the description of such a "falling in love"—it is a region from which no creature returns afterwards. One is never the same again.[16]

"It is an irreducible fact," comments Shideler, "and although reason can attack its appropriateness, its importance, or the conclusions drawn from it, it cannot deny to the experience its existence.[17]

Of greatest importance to the understanding of Dante's love for Beatrice is that the beloved is perceived "as a whole being significant of a greater whole." [18] This occurs when the whole person perceived becomes an image. When Beatrice dies, then her uniqueness appears to Dante as a quality independent of his love for her. There is a greater whole. "The experience—the sight, that is, of the beloved—arouses a sense of intense significance, a sense that an explanation of the whole universe is being offered, and indeed in some sense understood.[19] But, we ask, in what specific way is this true for Dante? "This is the identity of the Image with that beyond the Image. Beatrice is the Image and the foretaste of salvation."[20] "This identity justifies the lover when he speaks of his beloved as adorable; it vindicates his impulse to treat her with the reverential awe with which one is expected to approach the divine."[21] As the God-bearing image she is the "mother of love." Dante sees archetypal love within its type, Beatrice, the two realities interpenetrating each other.

As illustrated in the experience of Dante, adoration depends upon the lover's capacity for abstraction, for imaginatively perceiving an image, for living upon the plane of images where the innermost image of perfection is projected upon the real image of the beloved. This image is more real than her real person. Many expressive actions normally impossible become possible to the lover in adoration. Comments Benoit, "Strange that sometimes the loss of the person does not seem to affect the lover as would be thought by the intensity of his adoration, but it is adoration that accounts for this, for adoration is an image within himself, and is less dependent upon the presence of the beloved than would be supposed."[22]

True to the romantic ideal, says Benoit, "no adoration is possible without impediments, and if circumstances do not provide these, you find that the lover creates them, consciously or not."[23] No finer illustration in all literature is available to us than that of Dante and Beatrice.

The Renaissance—Marriage for Love?

The Renaissance period denied the existence of love in marriage, except by accident, as did the nobility of the seventeenth and eighteenth centuries in Spain, France, Austria, and neighboring countries. However, the idea of love in marriage was taking root during this time, and the English novelist Samuel Richardson (1689–1761) is credited with being the first to say that love was necessary for marriage.[24] Although arranged marriages necessarily dominated, a number of writers called for love and freedom of choice as the chief basis of marriage. In *The Book of the Courtier,* Castiglione advocated that one should love only a person one could marry. Nor was this altogether radical, as Andreas Capellanus had said the same thing more than 300 years before.

For Shakespeare not only is love the true basis of a relationship between the sexes, but a declaration of love is tantamount to a proposal of marriage. Although his lovers typically fall in love at first sight, they never yield to passion until they have pledged their troth. Despite her passion for Romeo, Juliet says:

If that thy bent of love be honorable,
Thy purpose marriage, send me word tomorrow
By one that I'll procure to come to thee,
Where and what time thou wilt perform the rite.[25]

Romeo and Juliet Act 11, Scene 2, Line 143

Shakespeare's message that the young should marry whom they choose and that they not bow to parental wishes is repeatedly conveyed in *A Midsummer Night's Dream, The Winter's Tale,* and elsewhere.[26]

Curiously, it was remarriage that offered the closest approximation to love matches. Because nearly half the English aristrocratic women died before the age of fifty, there was ample opportunity for men to choose a second partner.[27] And perhaps it was the handwriting on the wall that led the minister of Queen Elizabeth, Lord Burghley, to caution his son, Robert Cecil, "Marry thy daughters in time lest they marry themselves."[28]

Murstein's conclusion is, "The period from 1500 to 1615 was marked by significant advances in the freedom of choice of marital partners. In the early Middle Ages, par-

ents arranged marriages for their children without con-
sulting them. In the later Middle Ages, the Church insist-
ed on free consent of the parties involved, which in
practice gave the children a veto over parental choice. In
the sixteenth century, the children themselves began to
take a somewhat more active role in the selection of a
spouse, with veto power usually retained by the parents.
After the Council of Trent ruling, however, parental consent could be dispensed with after adulthood had been
reached."[29] So the Renaissance, while not leading directly
to the connection of romantic love with marriage, saw the
new concept gaining ground. Morton Hunt argues in *The
Natural History of Love* that the adulterous flirtation and il-
licit infatuation of the Middle Ages were the very instru-
ments that began to enhance woman's status and, hence,
eventually to alter marriage.[30] It seems, then, that the
place of romantic love in every major period of history
from the Greeks and Romans on cannot be denied. And,
interestingly, the dynamics seem to change little with the
changing times.

The Romantic and Victorian Eras

As the Age of Reason died in the mid-eighteenth century, a new movement—Romanticism—emerged and ex-
hibited its own special characteristics. The Romanticist
idealized what was natural, cherishing human emotion
and sensation as essential to fulness of life. It was human,
hence good, to entertain opposing feelings, to view life in
terms of antitheses. It was right to revere what was idio-
syncratic with respect to individuals. Romanticism was in
some ways similar to courtly love in its attempt to fuse the

sensual and the pure. Romanticism was also characterized
by protest, by rebellion against convention, especially
conventional morality. Though we tend to think sponta-
neity is a rather modern trend in the youth culture of our
day, Romanticism, too, had respect for the situation, the
immediate.

Along with veneration of nature was a focus upon the
terminus of nature—death. Death was related to the pure
love between the sexes, for death pointed to the Eternal.
This idea was focused in a German novel that fascinated a
wide segment of the population, Goethe's *The Sorrows of
Young Werther* (1774).[31] Here is the story of a young man's
passionate love for a young woman, named Lotte, who is
married to Werther's friend.

When Werther comes to see Lotte at her home on what
is to be their last night together, the two share their love
with deepest passion. In confusion and distress over the
conflict of her love for Werther and her feelings of loyalty
for his friend Albert, whom she honors, Lotte cries out to
Werther as she leaves quite precipitously, "This is the last
time, Werther! You shall not see me again!" And plead as
he will for one final word of farewell, Werther is not to
see her again. Later, at home, he writes her his farewell as
he plans to take his life. His letter is filled with ecstatic
raptures, passionate longing, doubt, and despair:

> Oh, I knew that you loved me, knew from the first soulful
> glances, the first hand pressure, and yet when I went
> away again, when I saw Albert at your side, I again de-
> spaired with feverish doubtings. . . . All this is transitory,
> but no eternity can extinguish the glowing essence that I
> imbibed yesterday from your lips, that I feel within me.
> She loves me! This arm has embraced her, these lips have

trembled on her lips, this mouth has stammered against hers. You are mine! Yes, Lotte, for ever!

And what does this mean, that Albert is your husband? Husband!—that is *to say*, in this world—and in this world it is a sin that I love you, that I would like to snatch you from his arms into mine? . . .

I go ahead! to my Father and to yours. To Him I will bring my plaint, and He will solace me till you come and I can fly to you, clasp you, stay with you before the face of the Infinite in an eternal embrace. We *shall* exist! We shall see one another again!

Werther sends his servant to Albert with a note requesting the use of two pistols to take on a journey. Upon receiving the note, Albert turns to Lotte and says, "Give him the pistols. I wish him good journey." Werther takes the pistols with a transport of delight when he hears that they had been handed to his servant by Lotte herself:

> I kiss them a thousand times for you have touched them. Thou, Spirit of Heaven, dost favour my resolve! And you, Lotte, offer me the weapon, you, at whose hands I wished to encounter death and alas, now encounter it. Here, Lotte! I do not shudder to take the dread cold cup from which I am to drink the ecstasy of death! It is you who have handed it to me, and I do not fear. Thus are all the desires and hopes of my life fulfilled!

The shot is fired, the body found; Albert and Lotte come to witness the last breath. The passion of love has mingled with doubt, despair, death. Werther is convinced of one thing: He shall have his beloved in Paradise.

Like Young Werther, the Romanticist viewed nature and destiny as taking precedence over bourgeois conventionality. Yes, lovers should feel free to defy unnatural human laws and to rebel against all human authority where it so intervened. Eternity shall vindicate those who truly love despite all earthly obstacles. This notion was epitomized by Werther. It was a dangerous new dimension!

There seems little evidence that the Victorian middle-class attempt to fuse Romanticism with conventional marriage succeeded. The passion of love did not integrate with middle-class morality. After all, Victorian mores called for the restraint of passion prior to and outside of marriage, even strong control within marriage. The Victorian man was a patriarchal figure, strong and masculine, combining reserve with passionless demeanor. At the same time, prudishness characterized sexual manners, so that expressiveness was largely inhibited in the culture of love. Women were expected to play the role of complete subordination to their husbands. And, worst of all, married women were expected to be sexless, free from all sensuality. In such a climate romantic love suffered something of a hiatus. What we customarily blame on the Puritans in American is better attributed to the Victorian legacy.

The Nineteenth and Twentieth Centuries

Compatible with the new freedoms for the individual—freedoms now prized by the rising middle class—was the special freedom to choose a mate for love. The universal triumph of individualism seemed achieved in this possibility of choice. Thus was romantic love brought into an unlikely merger with marriage. Love was now a choice dictated by passion and idealization. Psychologist Charles

Frankel notes, "When the middle classes took the world, they took over romantic love and domesticated it. It was conceived as an emotion properly felt only between two otherwise uncommitted individuals, and the proper prelude to marriage. In short, romantic love, which began as an aristocratic affair providing an outlet from marriage, has ended as a plebian affair which, in theory, is the only good reason for marriage. The cult of romantic love caps and sanctifies the great transformation of marriage in Western society."[32]

Middle-class women were emerging into new social roles and into a variety of occupations outside the home. The nineteenth century saw the rise of industrialism and the urbanization of life. Women left the home to join men in the factories and mills. But it was not until our century and the need for workers to fill the positions of men who were drafted for World War I that women began to take positions commensurate with their greater skills and improving education. Economic independence was the condition of social independence, and women had a greater basis for a major choice of their lives—to marry or not to marry.

World War II and the years that followed saw the rise of the new feminism and greater opportunities for women to become educationally, socially, and economically emancipated. Apartment living and public transportation, followed shortly by the advent of women driving their own cars all pointed to the decreasing domination of women by men.

Women's new choice was men's new challenge. Men and women found themselves strangers to one another in the impersonal masses that populated the cities. Means had to be devised for them to meet and get acquainted. Individuals were removed more and more from families and neighborhoods. Places of public entertainment rose to fill the need. The automobile became the means of private courting, and with romantic songs coming over every car radio, couples found they had romantic trysting places. Urban culture was promoting romantic involvements.

As women were moving away from the standard stereotype—housewife—so men were caught up in their own changing roles. The growing freedom of the sexes to associate together, especially to spend leisure time together, provided the opportunity for experimenting with new sex roles. Unchaperoned dating was now the vogue. Permissiveness was increasing as social constraints declined in the face of mass society. World War II ended with returning soldiers bringing back European ways of love, a greater sexual permissiveness than America had previously known. And an accelerating technology aided the evolution of romantic attachments. Popular and inexpensively printed romantic novels and serialized romances in the dailies carried the message to the masses. Radio throbbed with the love songs of the day. Movies and dance halls took their place in American life, supplying the major places for romantic entertainment.

The Influence of Hollywood

The formation of a romantic tradition in the United States is in many ways the story of the Hollywood film industry. To minimize its influence would be an injustice to the power of this dramatic art form. In the early days, beginning with the silent screen, romances and romantic film stars gave an aura of special excitement to a hard-working, more prosaic American public. Leading men and women were objects of secret adoration by millions. Stardom was based on the ability to portray a romantic figure successfully. This is what the people wanted, and this is what the people got. The stars in their film adventures, if not in their private lives, epitomized the dreams of most American boys and girls who reached adolescence. Watchers of the box office soon determined that nothing was more appealing than romance. War movies and westerns had to be strongly laced with romantic adventure. Nothing could compete with the excitement of furtive love trysts, obstacles to love being overcome by the popular stars. Nothing seemed to grip the emotions of men and women like the passionate fadeouts, the subtle suggestions of sexual romance, and even the final separations that turned many a romance into the most wrenching of human tragedies. Sexual and highly emotional love became the norm for the decades ahead, up to and including our own.

In more recent times new and sophisticated themes have appeared. What has gained major prominence? We would have to mention explicit sex, complex crime plots, technologically sophisticated settings, and every imaginable form of violence. Romantic relationships as such are no longer the dominant theme. But make no mistake; for all that is novel and bizarre, for all that is highly complex and sophisticated, romantic love is still present and a necessary element.

It is of interest to reflect on the numbers of Hollywood plots that end with marriage. The goal has been reached; the couple are now assumed to live "happily ever after."

Wedded bliss follows the romantic consummation in a sort of protracted romantic adventure unaltered by bills, budgets, and babies. It is never suggested that routine ruins romance, rather, it lends credence to the myth that romance overcomes all obstacles, even financial losses and physical disability, in-law discord, or unresolvable differences. The panacea is very simple in these plots: just find a true romance!

European viewers have occasionally called attention to the lack of realism of this Hollywood fare. Yet the basic motif has not changed much over time; it is perpetuated as television reruns and given contemporary settings.

Even the sexual revolution, on its way from World War II and all but complete in out time, failed to deromanticize love. For if, as it has happened, common access to sex partners has not diminished the passions of unfulfilled desire and even the need for the rituals of seduction, there remains a need. What shall excite the passions of men and women now if not a romantic love? So here we are—back to emotional needs of men and women and back to the wistful promise of romantic love to fulfill those needs. Romantic love doesn't die easily! The game goes on, luring new players, making the same promises, albeit in new settings.

In fact, the sexual revolution may well have enhanced our national need for romantic involvements. More than ever we preserve the myth that romantic love is a precondition to a happy and enduring married love. And to those growing numbers who are wary of marriage, who question any expectation of its being successful, living together without marriage appears to be the way to stabilize the passions of love and give some reasonable promise of continuance over time. At least they have seen that both the strength and weakness of American marriage is its basis in romantic love. For the majority of men and women the contemporary ideal of marriage remains, however, romantic, and there is little to suggest that this cultural ideal will change in the forseeable future. Romantic love persists as the universally expected essence of a good marriage. Countless marriages collapse when the myth fails. Blessed are those who learn that it is committed, caring love, not romantic passion, that sustains marriage. An intriguing thought that we shall pursue later is that it is marriage that sustains love not love that sustains marriage. Could this possibly be?

Our Changing Values

Perversely, in the contemporary public values it is marriage not romance that is regarded a snare and delusion; or in sociologist Mervyn Cadwallader's words, "a wretched institution."[29] Romantic seduction lives on but is more and more restricted to liaisons outside of marriage, where intrigue and deception can excite it all the more. What is more exciting than a secret affair? And if this were not sad enough, today the imagination is too jaded to limit romance simply to adulterous liaisons, every deviant form is utilized to titillate the imagination. The American leisure industry brooks no limits in devising attractions to secure box-office dollars. Deep within the American temperament there seems to be an insatiable need for romantic fantasy to lift us out of our drab selves and into that which promises to combine sex, emotion, and adventure. Here is one of the surer ways to go on a personally tailored ego-trip with all the alluring props culture and technology can supply.

In the mid-forties the prominent psychoanalyst Theodor Reik developed the notion that it was women who first devised romantic love out of their oppressed state.[33] Looking back over the past couple of centuries, Reik says that formerly men preferred their own company; women were appreciated and utilized as sex objects and as assistants in men's work as homemakers or in business and industry. Men were satisfied with mere possession and domination of women. There was little emotional tension, little ground for jealousy before or after marriage. Until more recent times women generally didn't have the individual significance that merited any great competition over them. It required an era in which women were more educated and socially liberated, when they could take more initiative and thus become objects of men's longing. A man's fantasy then could be preoccupied, especially with a woman who held him off or left him uncertain of her response. There was also an increasing variety of feminine types to compete for. Women, says Reik, found they could create a situation in which all the emotional possibilities for desire, yearning, tension, jealousy, and the like were present. A man had to woo and win his woman. Her refusal to surrender except on her own terms was now a possibility, for she was emancipated as never before, and she was no longer totally dependent upon some man. To be loved and appreciated, to be the object of affection and the partner in a commitment—this became the necessary premise for a woman to give herself to a man. According to Reik, this at least partially contributed to the rise of romantic emotion, and I agree with him.

Now, at long last, men must become lovers instead of sexually excited animals or demanding and domineering conquerors. Reik saw that romance is not a consequence of sex but coexists in tension with it; the two go together but are separate processes. He says, "Women became powerful only after men had begun to daydream of them; for, after all, they are much more seductive in fantasies than in reality."

In the process of men's learning affection—longing for women as significant, sought-after persons—women themselves were enabled to experience these same feelings and longings. Reik concludes, "Being loved gave women a new dignity and security, awakened new forces in them, and made them more beautiful and lovable as well."

Historically, then, we can confidently say that romantic love is here to stay. Modern social conditions will continue to perpetuate it. Only forms and contexts change; the dynamics remain the same. The need of individual men and women remains both personal and social, arising within the self, and expressing the need for special self-affirmation from an attractive and significant person. The extreme form of this affirmation, so desperately needed by so many, is romantic affirmation, adoration by a person of the opposite sex.

In other words, our egos need the exceptional nurture of a person in whose worshipful eyes we see our wished-for selves. We want to be significant in the eyes of one we consider attractive. Usually this means a continuing relationship, an intimate union within which we can persuade ourselves of our own attractiveness. Whoever is party to this accomplishment represents more than an individual; he or she stands for that whole other half of humanity now affirming our desirability! What a wonderful person this is! Thus we do find our lonely, alienated selves consoled and elevated to a new joy and a new sense of worth! We gladly return the favor by projecting attributes of worth upon the other party. Thus, too, we build self-esteem by means of another. Romantic involvement does indeed seem to add a whole new dimension to life. Should we not praise it?

This chapter has only touched upon the history of the rise of romantic love. It is a fascinating story, and for those who are interested in tracing this history in greater detail, three books are especially recommended—Morton Hunt's *The Natural History of Love;* Bernard Murstein's *Love, Sex, and Marriage Through the Ages;* and Denis de Rougemont's *Love in the Western World.*[34] In volumes such as these the story is fully told.

It's far too early to predict the demise of romantic love in American culture. And if my observations as a member of the counseling staff of a liberal arts college are any indication at all, the attraction to and intricacies of romantic attachment still hold sway on the American campus. But these are bodies of more open and questioning young people. They are more apt to study the sociopsychological dynamics that take place in their relationships than were their parents. They wonder all the more as they see their parents still very much romantically inclined, sometimes to the point of destroying a good marriage in the name of love. So the evolution of romantic love is not finished. Our generation shall write its own chapter in the continuing history.

Of All Themes Most Entrancing

'Tis that delightsome transport we can feel,
Which painters cannot paint, nor words reveal,
Nor any art we know of can conceal.

THOMAS PAINE, *What Is Love?*

*H*OW SHOULD I love you? Who shall tell me how? Today we live in the age of popular psychology, and we look to professionals in this field to give us direction. Self-esteem, self-assertion, coping, conflict resolution—whatever our psychological need there is a self-help book available. It's a billion-dollar business and growing each day. But who satisfied this ever-present need before the advent of professional psychology and the almost endless outgrowth of therapeutic agencies? Another way to ask the question is: What books filled the shelves of our bookstores and adorned our coffee tables then? For some three centuries it was the novelists who captured the popular fancy. They determined our understanding of the way love is.

Nothing is more fascinating to the student of love than to trace its features in a particular period of history and in the literature that pulsates with the love culture of the time. Have there ever been keener observers of the rhythms of love and hate, joy and sorrow, triumph and tragedy than the poets and novelists? Philosophers of old and psychologists of late never seem so clear sighted and natively intuitive about such matters as their contemporaries, the writers. It is that special genre of writers, the romantic novelists, who have captured a need deeply entrenched in the human spirit—the need for a passionate yet committed love relationship. Of course, the romances read by multitudes of people are often larger than life itself, with the effect that they create a climate of rising expectations. Unfortunately, these expectations are incapable of total fulfillment in even the most notable attempts.

Novels and Self-Fulfilling Prophecies

Romantic love received its most convincing validation in the romantic novels of an earlier day. To a considerable extent they gave rise to what we now commonly describe as a self-fulfilling prophecy. First, an expectation is stimulated; we come to expect something that normally lies outside the occurrences we've come to embrace. And who better than the novelists can stimulate such expectations in the matter of love! Then those in whom the expectation has been created unconsciously bring about the conditions that make possible an actual fulfillment of the expectation. Often, all that is required is some initial suggestion, some stimulus. With nothing more than an emerging expectation, the process of fulfillment is set in motion. Whether novelists of seventeenth-century France, as we shall be observing, or moviemakers of twentieth-century America, the possibilities exist for the creation of all kinds of self-fulfilling prophecies having to do with romantic adventure. A series of events is imaginatively devised, only to be moved in the direction of some romantic tension, some possibility for love to be consummated. Whether the resolution of that tension is in the form of triumph or of tragedy, either ending is immensely stimulating to the emotions and aspirations of those who are imaginatively able to identify their own desires with the plot.

The fertile imagination of the novelist depicts more romance than is ever experienced by living men and women, or experienced only in rare instances. But those who read romantic novels are often people with deep love needs, people predisposed to respond to the imaginary scripts by seeking to live them out vicariously. If they allowed themselves to think about it dispassionately, most might suspect that these stories belong to the world of make-believe. Nonetheless, they're reluctant to dismiss them or even to acknowledge to themselves that these romances speak to their own special love needs.

Bound to the necessities of sustaining life through labor and through the constant improvising of social relationships, the human spirit is a jaded spirit. The drudgeries and pressures of life take their toll. But romance quickens the imagination with the promise of a more pleasurable, exciting, and fulfilling world. Escapist it may be, but it is nonetheless attractive to masses of people. So, however veiled, these are hungers of the human spirit that reach out yearningly to the promise romantic involvement seems to offer.

From the many examples of romantic love in French, German and English literature we shall confine our brief exposure to a few significant French novels from the early seventeenth to the early twentieth centuries.

The great romantic novels were written when romantic love began to flourish in France in the seventeenth century, continuing on into the twentieth. Romantic literature succeeded in fusing romantic emotion with sexual passion, forming a complex set of need and fulfillment that then was assumed to be a compelling if not universal pattern. Descriptive analysis of the romantic passion into which French writers delved so deeply in this period has influenced our thinking up to the present. Typical of this major influence is Stendhal's seven stages of love. We shall take a brief look at Stendhal later on.

Until quite recently psychologists have been reluctant to consider romantic love a theme worthy of serious scientific study. This has changed with the studies of Elaine Walster, Zick Rubin, Vernon Grant, and a few others. Andre Maurois, a modern French literary critic, examines the sentiment of love in the life and literature of the seventeenth to the twentieth centuries in *The Seven Faces of Love*.[1] In the following brief analysis I shall, in effect, encapsulate the insights of Maurois, combining them with a few insights of my own.

L'Astrée first captured the attention of French readers in the early seventeenth century, teaching the exalted position women were to have with men. This place and power of women called for a certain formulation of the male response. Honoré d'Urfés *L'Astrée* painted the model for lovers. The so-called laws of Celadon, the hero, were actually those of romantic love: One must (1) love to excess; (2) have no other passion but one's love; (3) love one woman only; (4) have the sole ambition to please the

woman one loves; (5) defend one's shepherdess; (6) find
her perfect in every way; (7) have no other will but hers;
and (8) promise to love her always. Blaise Pascal, who
wrote during the same period, observed that "passion cannot be beautiful without excess. . . .When one does not
love too much, one does not love enough."[2] Lovers were
to sacrifice all to achieve such a love. The initiation of
love, of course, was always the man's.

The Heroic Ideal: Love Restrained by Honor

The heroic ideal common to the Middle Ages, as Maurois observes, was finally no longer able to express itself
through deeds of war and so sought its demonstration in
deeds and sentiments of love—quite a natural transfer-
ence in those changing times. These passions were ana-
lyzed by the writer of the famous *Maxims*, La Rochefou-
cauld, as the residue of self-love, and in this he was
astutely close to target. But the heroic ideal, applied to the
passions of love, produced its masterpiece in *The Princess
of Cleves*, written in the latter half of the seventeenth century by Madame de La Fayette. She was also among the
first in her time to depict a leisure society, describing with
exactness the sentiment that develop among men and
women when they have time on their hands and no other
occupation than the call of love. At the heart of *The Princess of Cleves* is the conflict between love and duty, passion in conflict with heroic pride of restraint. There must
be honor and sacrifice if love is true. It is love's passion restrained for honor's sake. Love is appropriately checked
by duty and honor.

Pleasurable Love—Free and Bold

In the eighteenth century heroic love checked by honor and supported by sacrifice was replaced by love as pleasure. Jean-Jacques Rousseau gave the world *The New Heloise,* so titled because it is, like the adventure of the medieval lovers Heloise and Abelard, that of a tutor who falls in love with the young woman entrusted to him. *The New Heloise* transformed the ways of love for at least half a century. No longer restrained by honor, love is free and bold, no longer sustained in secrecy, but out in the open, duty be damned. Here the illusions of romantics, their daytime languors and feverish, tormented nights, are all descriptive of the passions of love on the loose—unrestrained and also uncertain of any lasting satisfaction. Rousseau gave it focus in his words, "One enjoys, not what one obtains but what one hopes for, and one is happy only before being happy." This is the passion of anticipated fulfillment, with pleasure as the reigning principle. As we will see, romantic passion builds by anticipation, when the unfettered imagination can soar above the realities soon to be experienced.

Rousseau himself claimed to have loved only once, but he named two women whom he loved ecstatically: Madame de Warrens and the Countess d'Houdetot. He met Madame de Warrens when he was fifteen years old and she a comely twenty-eight-year old who had run away from an unhappy marriage. He stayed in her home for several years, and it was she who initiated the virginal youth into the sacred rites of Venus when he was twenty-one. He cried throughout the whole performance, and was later to write, "I loved her too much to desire her."[3]

At forty-five Rousseau loved the thirty-year-old Countess d'Houdetot. He courted her unsuccessfully for three months. She felt she must be faithful to her lover, and so Rousseau got only a kiss. But what kiss! As Rousseau expressed it later, "This single kiss, this pernicious embrace, even before I received it, inflamed my blood to such a degree as to affect my head: my eyes were dazzled, my knees trembled . . . I was obliged to sit down; my whole frame was in inconceivable disorder, and I was upon the point of fainting."[4] Clearly, the Age of Reason had its examples of romantic love, with all the familiar dynamics we know today.

Love Held Check by Virtue

Not honor or duty but virtue—this is the new direction as one century merges into another. In the eighteenth century love as pleasure had ushered in a new era, but it was to be replaced. In *The New Heloise* we observe the change; here it is the struggle of love with virtue not merely honor, as in *The Princess of Cleves.* This came with powerful force in the wake of the licentiousness that developed in the eighteenth century as women more and more adopted the morality of men. The pendulum was swinging back once more in reaction to the permissiveness and immorality that flourished for awhile. As Maurois asks, what is more monotonous than licentiousness, more melancholy than the ceremonial of another conquest, especially for those who have played the game all their lives? In Rousseau that which brings serenity and joy is real virtue, love checked and defined by virtue. The appeal of love must always surpass sex.

Through the eighteenth century there runs a countering theme represented by the work of Laclos, *Dangerous Relations.* Maurois says that Rousseau was really running away from his time, that he pictured love as he wished it to be not as it was in reality. It was Laclos who more clearly saw his times, picturing love as men and women practiced it in their leisure. In *Dangerous Relations* Laclos is asking what one does when one has nothing else to do but make love. Here love is the game of pleasure again. But his accent is upon this hitherto unproclaimed aspect: It is a monotonous game, and a dismal monotony at that. At least *The New Heloise* portrayed love as a delirium of passion and did not call into question that most natural gratification. But while *The New Heloise* did not look beyond, *Dangerous Relations* did. Pleasure has a price to pay.

We have no problem understanding the popularity of *Dangerous Relations,* because France was on the eve of the Revolution, and the cynicism of the times was reflected in its cynical conception of love, rightly or wrongly identifying the passions of love that now were so popularized with a decadent nobility and its games of sensual pleasure in the name of love. In the eyes of many love could not be seen as anything more than the passions of romantic folly.

In Love with Love

Coming now to Stendhal (the pen name of Marie Henri Beyle), we meet the dreamer. But he is much more than that. His great significance is that of the analyst, distinguishing four forms of love and giving us his seven stages of love. For the time let it suffice to note that the only form of love that Stendhal considered true love is passionate love. In his famous chapter on "Crystallization,"[5] he shows how the mind of the lover adorns the beloved with a thousand perfections, going on from there to discover new perfections from everything it confronts and projecting these, too, upon the beloved. It is a first notice of what we have come to term the mechanism of projection. Passion builds upon projection.

Stendhal dreams of the delights of mutual passion with a "divine" woman. However, Stendhal cautions us that, if one truly experienced such a passion and remained at this stage of love, the soul would grow weary. Why? Because it grows weary of everything that is uniform, even that which is uniformly "divine," in Stendhal's sense of the term. From the vantage point of our more developed understanding, we look back at this true perception of Stendhal and label it the law of diminishing returns.

An important stage to mention in Stendhal's view of love that of *doubt*. After having conceived a passionate hope, the lover suddenly encounters some indifference in the beloved, which thrusts him into doubt as to his true prospects for happiness at last. He muses that to anticipate being with your beloved is a joy so great as to make all the moments of separation unendurable; to be forever separated is hell itself. So enraptured does one become that he excludes all other passions, sacrificing everything to this single passion. All prudence and pride are cast aside in utter disdain for anything but his passion. In this sacrifice there is nobility. Thus is the ancient observation of Plato brought into view in Stendal: Passion is inflamed by the presence of obstacles; this is the soul of passionate longing. Thus is passionate love a necessary and sufficient reason for loving; it motivates man's highest energies—his

passions. And to sacrifice for the great passion will, ideally, overcome all doubt at last. Passion, and sacrifice on its
behalf, is the winning combination. Is it not a familiar
theme of moderns—*Love conquers all!*

It can be said that many of the great heroes of literature
are men and women, all of them otherwise noble, who for
love's sake have deserted their duty or transgressed the
rules of God and man. Neither law nor convention could
stand in the way of the great passion. While acknowledging the claims of both, lovers choose to risk society's condemnation, even to the peril of their immortal souls. The
incredible fact seems to be that love retains some honor
even when it defies morality; in fact, *because* it defies morality. In the opinion of those deluded by it, love has some
privileged status. Its waywardness and even its madness
are extenuated. Love is granted an otherwise unimagina-
ble immunity. When emotional excess lifts one's acts to
devotion and sacrifice, then the lover is to be judged incomparably human in the highest terms; this obscures everything else, or at least mitigates the wrongdoing. The
great lovers are made to seem admirable in spite of their
transgressions and indiscretions. They seem, in fact, almost justified in acting as though love exempted them
from the ordinary laws of life. It is as though their love
were a law unto itself. In Chaucer's "Knight's Tale" Arcite
says, "Love is a greater law than man has ever given to
earthly man." This is the great illusion! And yet it reminds us of a contemporary drift that has beguiled many.
Here once more, though in a more sophisticated garb,
love is made the principle that overrides all other consid-
erations, even law and convention.

A growing number of Christian ethicists are emphasizing love as the guiding principle of interpersonal behavior, and especially of sexual relationships. In the early 1960s the term *situation ethics* came into prominence with the appearance of two books, Bishop John A. T. Robinson's *Honest To God*[6] and Joseph Fletcher's *Situation Ethics*.[7] Earlier, theologian Paul Tillich had written, "The law of love is the ultimate law because it is the negation of law; it is absolute because it concerns everything concrete. . . . The absolutism of love is its power to go into the concrete situation. . . ."[8] Bishop Robinson wrote, "Love alone, because, as it were, it has a built-in moral compass, enabling it to 'home' intuitively upon the deepest need of the other, can allow itself to be directed completely by the situation. . . . It is able to embrace an ethic of radical responsiveness, meeting every situation on its own merits, with no prescriptive laws" (p. 115). Fletcher followed by writing, "Christian situation ethics has only one norm or principle or law (call it what you will) that is binding and unexceptionable, always good and right regardless of the circumstances. That is 'love'—the *agape* of the summary commandment to love God and the neighbor. Everything else without exception, all laws and rules and principles and ideals and norms, are only *contingent,* only valid *if they happen* to serve love in any situation" (p. 30). Elsewhere he adds, "When we say that love is always good, what we mean is that whatever is loving in any particular situation is good!" (p. 61).

Critics suggest a certain naivete in the supposition that love has a kind of built-in homing device leading us infallibly to its true goal. The very problem of determining just what love involves makes it clear that "love" is an uncertain guide. Love's path is not self-evident, and there is great uncertainty whenever love is made the final arbiter of what is right. Sentiment and desire can cloud the issue, for love is highly subjective and individual, and therefore inadequate to determine issues that are not individual but social in nature. Our human love may be distorted by ego interest or ego annihilation, sex dominance, or some other subconscious principle. Fallible people dealing with complex ethical situations, situations in which the consequences of a particular action cannot be fully foreseen, need more than love to guide them; they need principles, specific guidelines, moral laws. This is the biblical position. Love stands above law but not in contradiction to it. The law of love is not a substitute for the moral law, but a summary and a fulfillment of it. Commenting on this issue, ethicist Frederick Carney writes, "Even though Christians may be willing to be known as love-oriented persons, it is not love alone, strictly speaking, that serves as the complete principle of Christian moral orientation."[9] Love alone cannot penetrate to the underlying purposes of God that the Christian looks for in the order God has established for moral behavior, purposes sought in the biblical revelation. Philosophy professor Donald Evans points out that ethics is not simple, consisting only of love, but is extremely complex, with many different kinds of value to consider.

To young people in love, this formulation of situation ethics has a compelling appeal. But the love of which Joseph Fletcher speaks is the *agape* of the New Testament. So even if this kind of situation ethics were a safe guide, and I do not believe it is, young people are hardly mature enough in their understanding of *agape* to rely on this one principle of guidance. And when Fletcher says that "the

New Testament calls upon us to love people, not principles" (p. 64) this seems dangerously close to rejecting the
specific moral guidelines that the New Testament is so
careful to set down. So I would suggest that love is un-
questionably the highest principle for interpersonal relationships, but it does not stand alone. In view of Stendhal's position, the new morality is only the old morality
in contemporary dress. But, no; *"Love" is not the only ethical standard!*

Stendhal sees the beloved as perfect in every feature,
including piety, yet overcome by passion in dedication to
the great love. Even piety is overcome by the passion of
love; nothing at all in heaven or earth can withstand the
prior claims of love's passion!

So it is passion that makes love heaven when the beloved is there, hell when she is absent. It all reminds Maurois of Byron's earlier perception of the resourcefulness
that prevails in the intrigues of love, the bold courage that
appears at the height of passion. Stendhal wants it all; he
wants to encounter in women a bold contempt for all that
is not love. For him, only the sentiments of love are important. His theme is summed up in his words, "never be
afraid of the strength of your feelings."[10] He was indeed
ahead of his times, for the cry of the young today is little
different; it is a plea to let feelings be one's guide—one's
infallible guide.

Escape into Illusion

One of the most illustrious French novels was written
in the mid-nineteenth century by Gustave Flaubert—*Madame Bovary*. Emma Bovary incarnates the romantic illu-

sion; it is her escape from reality. She sees herself caught up with the imbecilic petty bourgeois, while out beyond lies the vast country of lush, expansive living—real living and real passions. Hers is the desire to escape to the "real" world.

Emma Bovary asks the young man, Leon, ardently, "Have you taken any walks in the neighborhood?" He replies that he goes and watches the sunset. "I think there is nothing so admirable as sunsets," she resumes, "but especially on the seashore." "Oh," says Leon, "I adore the sea!" And so it goes, from walks to sunsets to seashores—remarks that echo one another as these two romantics build upon a passionate sense of their oneness, a oneness created in the mind and upon nothing more substantial than coincidences. What a forewarning this gives of the way romantic pairs today give credence to coincidence as though it were the ultimate sign of their special identity.

Besides Leon there is Rudolphe, a vigorous man with a brutal temperament. He has many women but now finds Madame Bovary much to his liking. Emma's husband he appraises as stupid, so he decides on a conquest of Emma. For her part she is rather easily persuaded, for she responds out of her inability to throw off illusion. But Emma is after all, not unlike Rudolphe's other women. Yet Emma is to know at last the ecstasies of love, the fever of happiness for which she longed and of which she despaired. Hers is the delirium of passion; her whole being is caught up in the throes of the grand emotion. What else is worth living for? But for her lover, Rudolphe, Emma is no unique and sublime woman after all. He was merely attracted once more to a woman ready to be taken. The inaccessible is always a challenge, is it not? The charm of novelty, as always, falls away like a shed garment, laying bare the monotony of passion, which is seen to bear ever the same forms when exposed to the light of day. For Rudolphe even the novelty of novelty has worn off.

Up to this point Emma had placed her faith in romantic love. From here on the novel describes what becomes of the romantic woman for whom romance has failed. She can only numb her suffering in the diminishing pleasure, the transient, barren excitation of the senses. There is no more; love is not real after all.

For Flaubert romanticism is inevitable despite its illusory nature, its painful collapses. Does not everyone need to escape from himself? How better than through a romantic attachment? But this is to dream life not live it. So romanticism always fails; it pursues what is inaccessible, unreal. But once it has attained its goal, the goal evaporates; the inaccessible is now no different from everything else that is accessible. There are ever-present external circumstances, realities ready to crush the dream. Sorrowfully and pathetically, Emma ends in the clutches of Lheureux, reality's revenge. Emma's life is inexorably doomed to end in suicide, because the dream cannot coexist with daily life in the real world. In wanting the dream, she has refused life. Her husband Charles Bovary could have been the means of normal happiness had she been willing to accept the common joys, unromanticized, that Charles could provide her. But passion's false hopes prevented this.

Flaubert, it would seem, is too one-sided in his full condemnation of romantic love. My analysis shall not seek, as he does, to put life into "love-tight compartments," for to do so does violence to the whole of life as it integrates many facets seemingly contradictory to each other. There is a combining of the romantic with the real, the passionate with the more stable emotions. There is, in other words, more to passionate love than Flaubert discovers; others who follow shall make that discovery and cue us in. Yet he is devastatingly perceptive.

Later on in the nineteenth century, in times much like our own, other French novelists, such as Guy de Maupassant, Paul Bourget, and Anatole France, wrote voluptuously of adultery in high society. But one grows weary of the sameness of this theme. Then as now, purely sexual adultery cannot compete with the attractions inherent in the romantic encounter. Sexual passion may add its own kind of excitement to romantic passion but cannot compete with it when the two are taken separately. Stendhal had at least begun to see the psychological dynamics that make romantic love so appealing, so very entrancing and compelling. It is the romantic process itself that proves so exhilarating to those who are caught up in it, so intriguing to those who watch from without. Abstracting the process of romance from the actors in any particular situation, Stendhal shows that whenever certain conditions are present, a romantic pairing will occur, regardless of who the individuals happen to be. The romantic sequence need only be set in motion.

What Great Love Imagination Inspires!

Finally, Maurois comes to Marcel Proust, a novelist of the early twentieth century. Proust believes in the reality of love; that is, in the strength of feelings it inspires, the violence of sufferings it inflicts. He views passionate love as inevitable and fortuitous, as something existing in the mind of the lover rather than in the particular object of love. It is a malady, a mental aberration, and hence not to be justified by any exceptional qualities in the object, the person. The most vivid object is that which the mind creates.

In a story entitled "Swann in Love" Proust tells with great precision how these dynamics work. Swann is an art lover who enjoys searching the facial features painted by the masters in an attempt to recognize similar features belonging to people he knows, an innocent enough occupation. On one occasion, however, he is struck by the resemblance between the figure of Zephora in Botticelli's fresco in the Sistine Chapel and a woman named Odette. From this moment on the resemblance confers on Odette a beauty that translates for Swann into great significance for this otherwise insignificant woman.

The process of crystallization, as Stendhal would describe it, is now assured by this aesthetic link in the mind of Swann. So we see Swann going every night to Madame de Crecy's, where everything he observes has a charm that the presence of Odette confers. But Swann has certain doubts, as he sees Odette only at night. He knows nothing of her daily existence at all. To escape doubt somehow involves being closer to Odette in her daily rounds. So Swann frequents a rather vulgar circle that meets at the Verdurins'. Even that circle becomes acceptable to him because of Odette's presence. His critical faculties are no longer functioning, his powers of discrimination overwhelmed by his fascination with Odette. He is led astray by love! He is a hopeless victim of his own romantic passion, the captive of his own creation.

It is not physical possession so much as it is desire for emotional possession that has Swann enthralled. He is subject to great exaggeration, and his passion is raised by every element of curiosity that springs unbidden into his imagination. He suffers excruciating torments because, for all the uncertainties, the fastening upon the mediocre, the utter abandonment of critical discrimination for what he knows are only myths, he nevertheless has allowed this love to become everything for him. His will is now imprisoned. He is the captive of his inner world of idealization, intermittently able to see the less-than-ordinary quality of the woman upon whom he has fastened his love, yet unable to extricate himself from his fully developed passion. The *subjective* rules supreme over the *objective*.

In other words, as Proust portrays it, one can construct an imaginary being around a face or figure one has glimpsed only momentarily or from afar. In no time at all one has fallen in love, has started a process of idealization, or imaginary projections. The folly is simply that later on, when one has discovered the real person who is attached to that face or figure—with all the common features beneath the imaginary qualities—one continues to accept that person, retaining all the extravagant feelings born of the mental fiction. It is the incredible power of fixation. As we shall see in some depth later, this is an inexorable principle of all romantic involvement.

Proust seeks to show that love depends not on the quality of the loved one but on the emotions of the lover and on the circumstances that set the process in motion. Love is a need within the lover. We begin by being in love with love, which is a state of being. Then we cast about to see who it is we might be in love with. When at that propitious moment a likely actor walks onto center stage in our life, it happens. Often, then, it is a matter of chance that fills in the scenario with its chief actor. This "unique" man or woman could be replaced by any one of many possible others if the story had been located in another place and populated with other actors. For the process begins within us, issuing out of our own need. This particular person has merely stirred up all the emotions as longing within ourselves. It is we who endow the other person with the features we fall in love with. Precisely because we know so little about the other, we can fill in with our own imaginary creations. The mystery contained in the other triggers the movement in our imagination, a movement fueled by desire. This is all it takes.

The half-realization that complete possession of another is impossible, and the anxiety this generates, only intensify the desire and make it seem tragically noble to pursue such an impossible end. Proust saw that to strip our pleasures of imagination is to reduce them to nothingness. Yet the image must fade because of "the intermittences of the heart." At last the moment comes when the image can no longer be revived, can no longer be evoked in the depths of our spirits where they slumber. The love is dead; it died where it was born—in the lover's mind.

Is Emotion Forever Impervious to Reason?

Maurois' observations are equally applicable to our time, with its freedom of modern life, the common association of the sexes, and the degree of intimate interaction between them, all of which are conducive to a less idyllic but more healthy companionship of the sexes. Is the need for romantic experience less today? I think not. For we are an alienated people set adrift in the enormity and anonymity of mass society, overwhelmed by the impersonal faces around us. The urban way of life has isolated us within ourselves. Our psychological needs are not less but greater, for they are accentuated in an unrelenting culture of self-awareness. We wish for that which the hard realities of life seldom provide—community of persons, and the thrill of a romantic companion. We are bereft of the sentiments and passions of a great love, and we crave it. Possibly the only way in which multitudes of successful moderns can make an individual impact anywhere in their lifetime is romantically with another equally needy individual. Not that we are a people bereft of the intelligence that tells us the naked truth about such elusive love. It is rather that the most devastating analysis of the myths of romantic love are lost upon the human spirit so long as emotion remains impervious to reason.

The great French novelists exquisitely portray elements of the passion of love. Novelists of the nineteenth and twentieth centuries embellish their themes but add little light to the phenomenon; with this the critics agree. We shall turn principally to the psychologists and social critics of our time for an analysis of the forms romantic love takes in present-day culture.

The next chapter should prove especially helpful to young people looking toward marriage and to couples who may be agonizing over what seems to them an alarming loss of romance in their marriage. Against this background we can then more fully establish just what elements go into the other-centered, enduring, caring love that is more substantially suited to the promise of successful Christian marriage. It is my thesis that the New Testament holds the ultimate key. But since we are so culturally conditioned to accept a romantic view of love, so programmed to expect the unreal, the order of business for us must be an examination of the social and psychological dynamics of the love that dominates our social mythology and hence our lives. The radiance of caring love is more brilliant when seen against the dark foil of its romantic counterparts.

≈ 3

You're My
Magic Mirror

> The illusions of love may be sweeter, but who
> does not know that they are also less durable?
>
> CHODERLOS DE LACLOS, *Dangerous Liaisons*

Question: What is the difference between infatuation and love?

Teenage answer: Infatuation is when you think that he's as sexy as Robert Redford, as smart as Henry Kissinger, as noble as Ralph Nader, as funny as Woody Allen, and as athletic as Jimmy Conners. Love is when you realize that he's as sexy as Woody Allen, as smart as Jimmy Conners, as funny as Ralph Nader, as athletic as Henry Kissinger, and nothing like Robert Redford in any category—but you'll take him anyway.[1]

*I*NFATUATION is as different from love as fantasy is from reality. Although they are closely related, they should not to be confused, for that may mean deep trouble ahead. Whether we are thinking about teenage love or a mid-life affair, the difference is enormously important.

High on the list of questions in nearly any college circle is, "How do I know if it is real love or just romantic infatuation?" This question is further confused by those in the behavioral sciences, who question the reality of anything called love and who would explain it away entirely as a matter of ego-needs. Some professional psychologists seem inclined to dismiss love simply as little more than a waste of talent.[2] But romantic love is alive and highly visible in our society, playing a powerful role in countless personal relationships.

In marriage romantic myths continue to account for many of the disappointments, disillusionments, and marital disarray. Among the married extramarital *romantic* liaisons may be doing more damage than *sexual* infidelity. Emotional infidelity is often more critical in its outcome then sexual infidelity. Sexual passion and romantic passion are not the same and do not have the same consequences; they are very different, and their problems are distinct. Romantic involvement is the more critical of the two. Ask any husband or wife. For romantic involvement is more than lending the body to pleasure; it is giving the heart to another. This chapter will explore romantic involvement in the experience of both young people and those who, after years of marriage, may be threatened with the pull of a new romance.

Romantic Love and Infatuation

Romantic love is entrenched in American culture and has been for a century or more. Its effect upon contemporary life is not to be underestimated. A generation ago, Raoul De Sales, French journalist and astute observer of

American mores, wrote "America appears to be the only country in the world where love is a national problem."[3] More recently—and more temperately—sociologist William Kephart observed, "American has a special place in its heart for romantic love."[4] This seems more to the point. It is not too much to say that the heightened consciousness and the rising expectations of a generation devoted to self-realization have accentuated romance in love relations, and for understandable reasons. Not to experience romantic love constitutes a very real deprivation in our culture.

From childhood we've been conditioned to this philosophy of love relations. The national pastime seems to be mass participation in the sex-tease game of romance, if not in person at least vicariously by way of television and the movie screen. Slick magazines contribute their share. Nurtured by every cultural accoutrement, romantic liaisons of one sort or another offer the exotic hope of passionate adventure to a people who have everything and have tried everything, a people satiated and for whom nothing seems novel and exciting. What more is there when you've lived it all by age twenty? Only romantic love promises to banish the banality of our daily existence, giving in its place a fresh touch with something powerfully moving. So there continues to be a sense of entitlement that installs romantic love as one of the chief objectives in our grand pursuit of happiness. We feel entitled to at least one overwhelming romantic love involvement per lifetime. Then, no matter what, life has not cheated us.

Two myths persist: (1) that romantic love is the genuine thing, and (2) that love has a mystique quite beyond all power to analyze it. Love defies definition or analysis; it loses something in the translation, as it were. It is something that can be only experienced and described not scientifically scrutinized. For to analyze it is to lose it altogether. However, my premise is that to understand how love is generated is to be on guard against the dangers and deceptions that too often follow in its wake.

"How Do I Know if It's Infatuation?"

Romantic infatuation is, to use Dorothy Parker's phrase, "the gun you didn't know was loaded." Infatuation is just one of the many aspects of the phenomenon of romantic love. Infatuation appears as the initial stage of fascination, which draws two people toward one another. It is to a large degree irrational, obsessive, and overidealized. The term *infatuation* means to be carried away by irrational passions. The phenomenon has much to do with the sudden impact of a certain type of personal encounter between the sexes and with the desires and fantasies that almost immediately take over the personality of one or both of the parties. In some instances infatuation never proceeds beyond that initial encounter and the mere contemplation of the enchanting individual whom one never again meets in person. In adolescence especially no more than a fantasized relationship may exist, something that can live only in the mind. The beloved is simply someone to dream about.

Romance that begins with infatuation seems to thrive in situations in which someone is detached for a time from his or her usual circle of family and friends, temporarily freed from usual routines and responsibilities, somewhat at a loss as to what to do, and suddenly vulnerable to any romantic encounter. Sudden and acute loneliness can help set the stage. Perhaps it's a summer job away from college and home. For a married man it may be a week-long business convention far from his family. The situation may be highly conducive to exposing and taking advantage of a previously unrecognized need. Then, in the wake of a brief encounter, with every realization that time is short for the relationship to blossom, the infatuation acquires a desperate urgency, prompting the parties to even more excited, irrational behavior. One gets caught up in the emotion, little realizing that it is doomed because it is an artificial relationship being lived out in temporary circumstances and sustained by nothing more than a misplaced desire. And whenever an infatuation takes place in a particularly romantic, exotic setting, the individuals associate the enticement of the situation with the person who shared it. It is all very unreal, yet it seems completely real at the time.

Although infatuation is often identified with romantic love, as though the two were the same, we can see how distinct they are. Infatuation has to do with the irrational desires and passions that overwhelm two people who are suddenly carried away in an intense encounter. If a person has secretly wanted to fall in love, the immediate reaction to such an encounter is, "Maybe I'm in love!" or "I think this person is in love with me!" At the moment of impact, one tends to dismiss everything else from mind, and this is the danger of the enraptured moment. Nothing is more deceiving yet compelling! Infatuation is a happening; romantic love may extend its life.

Romance, Independence, and Alienation

Why is it that young people, from adolescence on, are prone to seek romantic attachments? Gail Sheehy caught it in her book *Passages:* "Love at eighteen is largely an attempt to find out who we are by listening to our own echo in the words of another. To hear how special and wonderful we are is endlessly enthralling. That's why young lovers can talk the night away or write fourteen-foot letters yet never seem to come to the end of a sentence."[5]

The fairy story most of us were raised on went something like this:

> I am a very attractive and lovable person, fascinating and desirable in every way. One day I shall no longer go unnoticed. The one and only person for me in all this universe will come along, and when he or she suddenly steps into my life, our eyes will meet and we'll know its for real. When we kiss, we'll know that we could not live without each other. Nothing will matter except that we are always together. We shall live for each other only; love will conquer every obstacle. Our love will be deathless; it will hold us in its powerful spell. We can know it's real, because we can't help ourselves; we are madly in love and couldn't be any happier. We feel we've known each other forever; everything about us merges with the other. We know then that love is bigger than we are, and we can't resist it.

Let's look closer and see what is really happening. Is that special person "my destinee," as in the theme song of the film *American Graffiti?* Or is love more of a natural thing that just grows and develops between young men and young women? What besides cultural conditioning creates this rather universal expectation of romantic encounters among our young?

One of the major developmental tasks facing all young people is that of making the transition from dependence upon parental love and family ties to independence and eventually to a love bond of their own. It's not an easy thing to go through this transition period, a veritable time between the times. At no period in life is the human need to love and to be loved stronger than now. For young people a romantic attachment is supremely an experience of being affirmed by another as an individual of worth and attractiveness. It is easy to fall for someone who affirms us, who esteems us, who values our company above all others and is attentive to our every thought. Imagine—an attractive person of the opposite sex attracted to me! What greater proof of my worth and lovableness? I always knew I was attractive; now I *really* know!

For a time a young person's very identity, having been severed from parental attachment, seems to hinge upon its being a shared identity with someone else, someone who is regarded as a significant person of the opposite sex. Often this need is accentuated by a sense of alienation that so many young people feel today—alienation from parents, sometimes from peers in a huge high school or college, or from social institutions they no longer feel at home with. In the transition to independence and maturity there is even a mysterious sense of alienation from parts of the self. One does not feel like a whole, completed person; the self is fragmented. There arises a need for something more than companionship with either sex; the need is for a love bond accompanied by a heightened

sense of self-affirmation. The lure of an emotionally intimate relationship, a pair bond, is its promise to meet a
number of personal needs at one stroke—the needs for affirmation of self, for devoted attention from a significant
person, for a new security and status, perhaps for someone to help us make the break from parental ties. For
many it will seem an instant answer to loneliness and social isolation. It is the adolescent's developmental needs
that make a romantic attachment appealing and compelling.

Romantic love is a context in which to test and develop
growing social skills such as communication skills. It is
also an opportune time in the period of adolescese when
young people can idealize each other to their heart's content. Exorbitant fantasies belong to this period of life, and
they can be entertained at a time when adults will more
readily accept them for what they are. Later on it will
have to be different because the consequences will be different. But for now, in an impersonal world fraught with
anxieties and uncertainties, a delightful possibility seems
to be a haven for two, a private world for two lovers
alone. Here is a very special kind of interpersonal experience like nothing else. It seems to provide a relationship
where two young people can gain something interperson-
ally for themselves that they feel is worth the effort they
put into it, something *they* can choose to experience. Here
they find an exhilarating degree of excitement and personal adventure, removed from parental involvement,
with no preconditions they have to meet and no commitments beyond the most minimal and most tentative. What
an inviting adventure romance affords to the young!

On the campus of a large university a pair bond offers

two young people a kind of special security in an otherwise somewhat overwhelming and isolating environment. It also has the secondary feature of being something of a compensation for these alienating hurts inflicted by a noncaring society that tends to engulf so many students. An additional role such romantic attachments serve is that of providing a community of two where young people find mutual support and reinforcement in their resistance to the values and expectations of parents. By retreating into the privacy of their relationship, a couple can withdraw from the social obligations with family and friends that are expected of them but which they no longer desire. As Philip Slater, an authority on the youth culture, expressed it, they "unite to withdraw" from the pressures of social life and from the conformities of home and community.

The Magic Mirror

For many working singles the bleak anonymity of their workday world brings with it a lost sense of integration into the larger society. Often there is also an accompanying boredom with much that makes up their daily work— a loss of pride in what one is doing to earn a living or a lack of personal involvement in what is no more than a routine job. For some singles work is only another alienating feature of modern life. There are few rewards for the human spirit. Consequently, working singles look to a love relation to supply those rewards. Happy are those who find it; unhappy are those who do not find it and settle instead for some pseudo-love.

In such circumstances a romantic attachment may seem

to offer the only adequate compensation, the only window from which one can look outside of an unhappy self. Whether a college student or a working single, the individual who is newly separated from home, community, and the social restraints both of these imposed is groping for the means to become a whole self, an integrated and completed self. A young woman may have been the last domain where her mother could play out her maternal role or her father could be the supreme model of masculinity. The sudden independence is confusing and unsettling. Or a young man may have achieved a large degree of independence, only to find himself uneasy as to how to use it. His sense of identity is similarly unsettled. In either case a new, quite unpredictable self is striving to emerge. That emergence is slow, somewhat painful, and not without anxiety. Deep within is the yearning, "Oh, for a mirror to reflect back my new image! Oh, that I might see what I am becoming!" And what more assuring mirror could be found anywhere than the adoring eyes of an attractive person of the opposite sex, a person who returns affection and affirmation? Is this not the magic mirror?

For a young woman to separate herself emotionally from her parents may be more wrenching than for a young man to do the same. But does she not have the advantage that she can accomplish this developmental task indirectly, simply by letting control of her life pass from parents to boyfriend? She may then presume that her commitment to him justifies, even demands, this shift of allegiance. Her boyfriend replaces her parents. Is this not what love requires? Seemingly, of course! If she is convinced that he is the one-and-only, then she finds no polarization at all between these two loyalties. Her new identity is completed in union with her boyfriend. In his eyes she sees, at last, the reflection of her new, completed self. What is this really? It's the magic mirror!

So often a young man has achieved a high degree of independence from his parents by this time; a young woman has not. The relationship primarily aids her in this endeavor.

Gail Fullerton, in *Survival in Marriage*, reviews the possibilities inherent in this developmental stage and suggests that, with the passing of time, a girl may recognize that her attachment to her boyfriend is not the real commitment she assumed it to be but a supporting role helping her make the transition away from her parental ties. Initially this was obscured from her mind because she had so readily taken to the relationship for its own sake. Unknowingly, she was looking to her young man to provide all the love and security, the parental deference she once had received in her family, while at the same time handing her a new identity. She doesn't recognize her deep yearnings are to have the adoration and special place of her childhood days reenacted once more through her lover.

If, at a later time, this young woman does recognize what has taken place, she may face a crisis and a difficult decision. Can she turn this dependency into a commitment? Is this man the one who can fulfill the long-range needs of her life in an enduring love? If not, what then? It happens only too often that by this time there is a sense of having invested so much in the relationship that to break it off would be traumatic. One is tempted to stay with it in hopes that a new foundation can be laid somehow. It is a time fraught with great danger—the temptation to not be hurt or to hurt by making the rational decision. It is easy to fall back into romantic illusions, into the formerly shared identity, into the comfort of a false hope. Courage is required to make the break.

If, on the contrary, a young woman has not experienced parental love, her longings are of a different sort altogether. Her needs rise out of love deprivation. She is looking for whoever can promise to make up in the present what has been missing in the past. It is a large order, this hope that the love she's never had will be realized in her romance, for she is building wholly upon a need within herself.

For singles the formula for the "new me" is all too often expected to be the outcome of some romantic affair. And, really, who of us doesn't at times feel the desire to become a new, more alive, and exciting self? Who of us doesn't get bored with the sameness of our self? And who of us has not at some time idealized himself or herself—in rather dramatic terms—into either an extraordinary lover or a beguiling beloved? Who hasn't entertained the secret claim, "I'm made for a great love; someday, suddenly it will come my way!" as though we only need to meet the right person, fall in love, and that person will hand us a new self. We'll be transformed as if by magic! Surely, we insist, beyond our tired, undramatic self there is, there must be, another more attractive self just waiting to be born. And what does it matter that this new self is largely an illusion if it enables us to escape the dull, prosaic routines of daily existence?

Romantic love is a magic mirror, a new way to see oneself. Any satisfying self-affirmation depends in part upon our having a mirror in which we can admire, and so be assured of, our own lovableness. This means having another person paired with us who reflects back that lovableness through affection and attention. Even better still is having that person constantly with us, especially in showcase situations, so others can also share our reflected attractiveness.

The magic mirror of romantic love throws back an image radically different from the image thrown back by parents, teachers, or close friends. This reflected image is what we most want to see in terms of our desirability where it matters most. We very much want to believe what this particular mirror gives back. But, similarly, should this mirror later fail to reflect the same much-desired image of ourself, reflecting instead a negative image of a person not loved, then the one who has been our magic mirror will have to be replaced and will have to get the blame for what has happened to break us up. The first principle of romantic love is this: The beloved's responsibility is to reflect back our wished-for self. In this respect, romantic love is little more than an ego-trip, with each giving credit to the other for the apparent miraculous self-transformation. It must be love! What else? And so goes the myth of the magic mirror.

To fall in love is to play the starring role so often seen on the screen, to pick up on the cues we've learned so well. It is to stage dramatic encounters of one's own, replete with all the ecstasies and agonies, the fateful suspenses, the passionate fadeouts. Such a scenario is tailored to feature a new, exciting *me* and the fated union of *us*.

Idealization and Projection

Idealization means seeing another person in the light of what we wish that person to be. *Projection* means taking an ideal image and mentally imposing it upon the other person. When we project, we superimpose the ideal image upon the real image. Both idealizing and projecting are expressed in a classic statement by the philosopher George Santayana: "The romantic lover is free to love what he imagines, and to worship what he creates." [6] Starting with only a partial picture of a person, the lover soon fills out the detail from his or her own imagination. This projecting of an ideal is sometimes referred to as "the halo effect."

For romantic passions to awaken, there must be something intriguing about the object of our love, something mysterious. Romantic love creates a mystique, and the question follows: What is the nature of this mystique?

To begin with, the opposite sex always creates a mystique. The aura of mystery that is the consequence of sexual differentiation is perhaps greatest for those who have grown up as an only child or who, by reason of age difference, have been removed from siblings of the opposite sex. Add the particular fascination of a person who is outwardly attractive but about whom little if anything is known, perhaps even much that is concealed. Elements of intrigue already present are heightened as one begins to idealize and project the person desired upon the actual person. The imagined lover or beloved is perceived as ideal, as always performing perfectly, and as fulfilling every expectation.

Typically, this process is facilitated when the romantic encounter takes place in what has become a rather standardized setting—two lovers withdrawing into their own type of privatism. The consequence is that they take little opportunity henceforth to observe each other in more extended circumstances, in those everyday situations where the less-than-ideal traits are more likely to rise to view. Such special circumstances tend to exclude the appearance of, say, normal frustrations, coping difficulties, or perhaps some behavioral excesses or deficiencies. Eventually, however, the unflattering light of continual association makes it difficult for either party to maintain an idealized image of either self or the other. A danger, nonetheless, is that the disenchanted partner will retain the illusion—"I'll change him. If I try, I know I can bring out the real person hidden within." Idealization and projection easily lead to deception and disillusionment.

Inwardly, the consciousness of imperfection drives some people toward perfection as a goal. Perfectionism is a self-deceiving state, and perfectionists are among the most difficult individuals to live with. An interesting variation of this is expressed in romantic attachments. Since the ideal of perfection cannot be actualized, we may imagine it as an aspect of ourselves, the perfect lover or beloved, or project it upon the one with whom we hope to identify in a pair bond. If we can possess the ideal loved one as our own, it is as though we assimilate his or her strengths and endowments.

Of course, idealization and projection place demands upon people that they cannot bear for long, demands in the form of expectations that otherwise would never be there. Unless two people recognize in time what is taking place, the relationship is bound to break down under the weight of these artificial assumptions.

Falling in love, then, happens when our imagination projects nonexistent attributes onto someone else, personal perfections we desire to assimilate to ourselves. However, if our feelings are to grow and mature into genuine, caring love, we must reduce these projections and scale down the idealizations so far as we are able, replacing them with the image of the real person. Then we can go on to unite our authentic being with the loved one's authentic being. Honest self-disclosure and the willingness to share in the widest set of circumstances is the key to exchanging idealization for a healthy realism.

Recently psychologists have pointed out that what romantic lovers long to possess are often attributes they do not possess but admire in another. These may be facets of the distinctive maleness or femaleness of the person to whom one is attracted. Sexual attraction in this sense is more than physical attraction. A young woman is fascinated by the masculine aspects missing in herself and alien to her own femaleness, aspects represented in her boyfriend. Likewise, a young man is fascinated by the feminine aspects missing in himself and alien to his own maleness, features with which his girlfriend is endowed. The more these facets shine forth from a particular individual, the more the lover is fascinated and drawn closer.

We can understand now why infatuation begins with such suddenness, with such impact. For one thing, it is captured attention—the focus and intrigue of a new and entrancing personality. From then on, imagination quickly takes over. The element of surprise adds excitement. Little beyond that is required to make the encounter as all-consuming as it was initially emotionally electrifying.

Two people who one moment are total strangers suddenly let the wall between them fall. The social and psychological distance is no longer a barrier. All at once there is what psychologist Erich Fromm calls "sudden intimacy."[7] Of course, the first response may evidence little more than the degree of loneliness and emotional hunger the two people are feeling. What happens then is simply what each of the two needs to have happen, and so each acts as a catalyst helping it happen for the other.

We know that sudden, unexpected changes in life arouse far more emotion and tension than do gradual, expected transitions. Under the right conditions, instant intimacy does seem to take place. Two people quickly can assume that they are not only *made* for each other, but *meant* for each other, that theirs is true love beyond any doubting.

The Body Language of Love

Albert Mehrabian, a contemporary behavioral scientist who has studied the importance of facial communication, concludes that roughly 55 percent of our communication signals are facial.[8] According to Mehrabian, romantic love depends very much on what he calls "facial invitations." This is not surprising, for facial features make up the richest area of physical individuality, providing a repertoire of expressions to attract others to ourselves. These features and expressions also provide wide differences between individuals from which a personal choice can be made. This is why there is so much visual preoccupation between lovers who gaze into each other's faces. It is the most direct route to achieving a vivid awareness of a loved one's singularity. (Years ago marriage educator David Mace wrote that if a couple spent their time doing nothing but gazing into each other's eyes, all they would develop is a squint!)

Romantic love usually includes a strong sexual attraction, so much so that some investigators have found difficulty in distinguishing the two. But romantic love differs in that its essence is not physical but aesthetic attraction. Falling in love is a response to such individually aesthetic traits as facial expression, especially what is expressed by the eyes and smile of a person. The case for this is well made by the psychologist Vernon Grant. When a young man speaks of "the light in her eyes," he is making an accurate observation. Whenever one person responds to another with excitement, the eyes "light up" quite literally. How inspiring to detect in another's eyes the signals of a willing response, a warm acceptance, a strong interest! To put it another way, the eyes reveal the extent to which someone is fascinated by the "charms"—real or imagined—of the attractive person. The very word is expressive—*charmed.* The eyes are indeed windows upon our inner feelings, which otherwise might be concealed. The eyes communicate in varied and subtle ways and, together with the expression of the mouth, convey worlds about a person's thoughts and feelings. It is easy to pick up an invitation or a rejection from such facial expressions.

Are we not all familiar with the following situation? The smile of a young man when he sees a young woman who attracts him is all but automatic, as he takes her in with a glance that leaves nothing out. Her blush and averted gaze then evidence that she knows he sees her. Her own response is expressed through sparkling eyes and flashing smile, a toss of the head, spontaneous laughing and body animation. It is the body language of love. What follows is the game of alternating advance and retreat. Small hints of interest are followed by mock indifference and modesty. The game takes on the impulse to chase and be chased but never quite to catch and be caught. All this is accompanied by the romantic line which, subtle as it may be, is readily recognized as a come-on and is still found to be most compelling. *Flirting* is the word for one of the more highly developed arts of the ages—a tantalizing way to express an invitation to further interest.

Teasing, which also plays a prominent role in romantic interaction, is commonly recognized as one of the main techniques by which romantic tension is stimulated to higher levels. Teasing tends to increase tension in the same way that laughing releases it. To tease one another is to play together, but it is a semiserious game. The two keep a certain social distance, while at the same time saying in a semiconcealed way, "I'm attracted to you. I won't let you catch me yet, but I dare you to try!"

Teasing can be great fun, for it keeps the relationship somewhat on the plane of a game, the plane of the superficial, sufficiently so that any more serious commitment is held in abeyance. Even mild insults are a way of teasing, of saying, "I love to make you pretend that you're angry with me, because I know full well you aren't, really. And anyway, it will be great fun melting your anger with an affectionate move." This is a stimulating way to put the relationship to an early test, to see if there is a response to romantic play. A young woman's pretended indifference has been known through the ages as *coyness*. If she is interested, she will play the game. If not, little is lost.

Is Love Blind?

A common expression is "Love is blind." How is this to be understood in the light of the process we've been studying? What we mean when we say that love is blind is that romantic love is subject to *selective perception*. Lovers see what they want to see in each other, filtering out what they do not wish to see. Or, in other words, beauty is in the eye of the beholder. Whenever someone says, "I don't understand what she sees in him," the answer is, "she sees what she wants to see. What *she* wants to see and what *you* see are two different things." And what does she want to see? Charming aspects, yes; blemishes, no. In this way the ideal characteristics are accentuated, the less-than-ideal features ingeniously kept all but invisible. So lovers, if not blind, are myopic; they are prone to selective perception.

Lovers often claim that they are completely open with one another, that they hide nothing. "We've only known each other two weeks, but we know all about each other. We've let it all hang out. Love doesn't hide anything, you know." Doesn't it? Lovers hold to this claim because, as they say, "Our souls are one." An immediate sense of shared identity creates this illusion. But the opposite is closer to the truth. The romantic stage of love is never really that open and candid, for both parties are intent upon maintaining good impressions—sufficiently so to keep the other interested and get the relationship off the ground. The image they want to project of themselves at this point is everything. Perhaps unconsciously they are following the wise principle: You never get a second chance to make a first impression.

Take Sandy and Bob, for example. Sandy seems especially faultless to Bob, because he sees only the image of her that he has idealized and projected upon her. Because a few of Sandy's characteristics are especially attractive, it is easy for Bob to assume that her entire personality is the same. Sandy encourages Bob's view of her by accentuating what he seems to like, concealing what may not fit his picture of her. And because his response further encourages her, she finds herself cultivating new and exciting self-potential. Bob is doing the same, and at first this is not too difficult for either of them.

Sandy and Bob are exhibiting only a part of themselves, the part that responds to the expectations of the other. If Sandy gets intimations that she is beautiful, she takes special care thereafter as to how she dresses and arranges her hair, although at other times she is inclined to be somewhat careless about her personal grooming. In fact, up to now she had thought it quite avant garde to be sloppy in her dress and grooming.

If Bob picks up intimations that Sandy considers him thoughtful and considerate, he will encourage this view by taking special care to do nice things for her, although in other relationships he may be quite thoughtless and inconsiderate. Each is trying to keep up the impression that pays off. When Bob whispers to Sandy, "I only want to do what pleases you," he may just mean, "I only want to do what keeps you impressed with me."

Both appearance and disposition can be remarkably improved simply by a beloved's intimations that one is attractive and kind. We might call this the Cinderella effect. Wanting it to be true, the individual strives to make it so. In the process he or she clings all the more tightly to the beloved as a prop for what hopefully will be a never-ending masquerade. This unconscious clinging and striving may eventually bring about a break-up. Unreality, in time, must give way to reality. The shock may be too great.

Will honest self-disclosure prevent a break-up? It all depends. No, if the pretense has been a highly effective technique up to this point. Yes, if the two have sufficient maturity to take what is genuine in the relationship and begin to build on it.

The Game of Ego-Enhancement

When a man finds a woman desirable romantically, she is able to think of herself as the desirable woman she always longed to be. Her thought is then, "What a wonderful man who has discovered how desirable I am!" Likewise, when a woman finds a man desirable, he is able to think of himself as the adequate male he always longed to be. His thought is then, "What a wonderful woman who has discovered how desirable I am!" At the very heart of it is ego-enhancement. Not that this is all bad; but this is the nature of the process. Whatever she expects him to be, he suddenly becomes all those things. And she the same. If he is enchanted to find someone who hangs on his every word, he will work at having an opinion on most things. If she is enchanted to find someone who adores everything about her, she will work at maintaining and improving the basis for it. It may not be love, but it may nonetheless have an important role in getting a relationship going. Even matching dependencies sometimes pay off!

Theodor Reik contended that all of us long to be special people. When we become painfully aware that we are not as special as we had hoped, we cast around for someone who is, someone whom we can at least regard as special. Then by attaching ourselves to that person, we share his or her importance. By making another person an accessory in this way, we acquire the specialness for ourselves. This, too, is a form of ego-enhancement by means of another person. If the relationship progresses beyond that stage, it may not have negative effects but may signal the beginning of something that will mature as time goes on. What is curious is the price some people are willing to pay in their attempt to establish relationships that cause them to feel so good about themselves! The apex is reached with a deeply romantic involvement.

How Self-Centered Is Romantic Love?

To a large extent, romantic attachment serves as a catalyst for generating self-love. Another individual is used as the means through which a person loves him- or herself; the other becomes a means to an end, not an end. Sometimes when a young man says, "I love you," he may really be saying—although unwittingly—"I love me, and I love the way you make me feel about myself." Or he may mean nothing more than, "I love having someone fall in love with me." Relationships of an intimate kind can be either comprehensive, total, interpersonal relationships, or they can represent only the most superficial touch two people can have. Recall young Augustine's words, "I love loving."

Even the words "I love you" can mean all kinds of things. To speak with great endearment may in fact reflect a need to picture oneself as a great and eloquent lover. One is enamoured with one's own words, actions, and emotions. Terms of endearment can have very subtle and hidden manipulative functions. The lover may use the language of love to camouflage an attitude of entitlement—"After all I've done for you, am I not entitled to your love?" But this is buying love, and love cannot be bought. Nor is it really love that tries to maneuver another into a position where demands can be made. Acts of giving can have motives of receiving. After all, love relations belong to an interpersonal exchange system that involves two ego-structures. The extravagant attention one gives to another may simply have been generated out of a fear of losing the cherished attachment. In such instances, losing the lover is not as crucial as losing the love!

The story is told of a very self-centered young woman in old Vienna. One day the psychiatrist Alfred Adler heard that she had fallen in love. He asked with a smile, "Against whom?" Such a question is appropriate to ask any self-centered lover—young woman or young man!

For a self-seeking individual falling in love may merely be opportunism, a way to prop up a sagging ego, or maybe just a bad habit. In other words, romantic love, for all its claims to the contrary, tends to be largely narcissistic—centered in self. For many, nonetheless, it is a rewarding expenditure of personal talent, calculated to reap a rich return of attention, thereby enhancing one's self-love. But any love worthy of the name must be more than this.

Neurosis Calling to Neurosis

Sometimes, of course, what passes for romantic love is no more than neurosis calling to neurosis. A neurotic person has a need to attach himself or herself to another as girlfriend or boyfriend. This and nothing more is what brings them together and keeps them together. It may be that one of them has a neurotic need to control someone else, while at the same time the other has a need to be controlled. Early childhood relationships can create these kinds of needs. Is it not a curious thing how similarly incapacitated individuals seem to gravitate to one another? In his insecurity sometimes the man wants someone who will never say no to him, who will do his bidding without question, and, hopefully, fulfill his every need. Not uncommonly a woman needs someone who will take over her life completely and so absolve her of all responsibility to think or act on her own. The man may need a mother-substitute, the woman a father-substitute. For them to indulge such neurotic needs is to allow their own past to blackmail them. Nothing is more futile than the attempt to find someone who will meet all the personality needs one has accumulated since childhood, which is, of course, sheer impossibility.

If a young partner in loving suspects an overattachment is in the making, one that may have neurotic overtones, he or she should as objectively as possible examine the relationship for such elements as extreme possessiveness, unrelieved exclusiveness, unreasonable demands, recurring jealousy and depression, and perhaps subtle forms of manipulation. A good question to ask is whether the other partner has a good capacity to give or is able only to receive. Does that partner seem especially dependent? Does nearly everything in his or her life seem to hinge upon the relationship? Is his or her presence a smothering presence? Any one of these conditions may indicate a neurotic need sufficient to indicate that the person does not have the capacity for caring love that an intimate partnership requires.

Another sign worthy of at least a brief mention is

that neurotic lovers are usually loath to grant their be-
loveds the right to be independent individuals in any
real sense, but insist they be only the lover's alter ego,
an extension of the lover's own self. One frequently
finds this unhealthy form of attachment among those
who attempt to keep a loved one apart from family or
friends as much as possible.

Yet another form of neurotic love is touched upon
by Rollo May, who remarked, "It not infrequently happens that two persons, feeling solitary and empty by
themselves, relate to each other in a kind of unspoken
bargain to keep each other from suffering loneliness."[9]
Every counselor has met young people troubled with a
love relation that can be described as neurosis calling
to neurosis, with little to commend its continuance.

The Cycle of Emotion, Passion, and Romance

Romantic courtship builds up around many little
shared experiences of a daily nature, leaving the parties increasingly involved with each other. Feelings
develop until both lovers are impressed with the depth
and intimacy that now characterizes their relationship.
So much has been confided, simply because two people
who need someone to confide in have found each other. More significantly, this is part of the developmental
task of shifting their dependencies from parents to
likely substitutes. The occasion for such confiding is afforded simply by their being together constantly and
by the exclusive nature of their pairing-off together.

Thrown together in an intimate way, the two act
upon each other emotionally; it cannot be otherwise.

As emotions build up in one of them, they are communicated to the other. The emotional climax of such sharing may reach great proportions. And since such emotions cry out for relief, for lovers this usually means channeling them into physical expressions. Then there is a mutual reinforcement between the emotional and the physical. Unless the two are aware of what is happening, the romantic aspect becomes much like addiction to drugs. The correlation is significant enough to be discussed in a recent book, *Love and Addiction.*[10] Emotional dependencies make for extraordinarily strong ties. But emotional addiction is not love.

Because the emotional interaction is pleasant just as physical interaction is pleasant, feelings of euphoria tend to dominate the whole relationship. What happens, then, if the relationship suffers a sudden withdrawal of one of the lovers? The chain of response is disrupted. The euphoria immediately dissipates and may be followed by emotional trauma, disorganization, loss of sleep and appetite, depression and confusion, and sometimes by a strong temptation toward destructive acts against either oneself or the other party. As quickly as emotional dependencies can develop, they can collapse. The more they have taken over the individual, the greater will be the sense of loss when emotional reinforcement is no longer present.

For our own protection we must recognize that romantic emotions are marked by idyllic peaks and dark valleys. Emotion reaches heights and plunges to depths. So if a mature love relationship is to develop, it will require a broader base than just the relating of two emotional centers. Emotional interdependency is proper in itself, improper only as it is excessive, driving a couple into themselves and precluding the normal development of other relationships.

Romantic Love as Esthetic Attraction

Romantic passion differs from sexual passion, although the two are closely associated. Modern psychology has shown the two to be polar opposites. Theorist Vernon Grant notes that poets and novelists have celebrated romantic love as something whose essence seems to lie in the realm of esthetics, and as such it has inspired creative works in all fields of art.[11] He distinquishes the esthetic and emotional aspects of sexual attraction, observing that a person in love is both esthetically and emotionally fixated on another person. "There is a tendency to dwell on esthetically attractive traits, on mannerisms, and style of personality" (p. 23). Grant distinguishes esthetic attraction from both emotional and sexual attraction, noting that the richest area of physical individuality is that of the facial features. These together with voice, bodily movements, and especially the expressiveness of the eyes are esthetically perceived characteristics that cause attraction. The emotional responses these characteristics arouse, says Grant, are more like the feelings associated with the appreciation of art: Another person is found esthetically pleasing. Grant cites George Santayana's *The Sense of Beauty*, in which he writes on the relationship of esthetics to sex. Grant recalls Schopenhauer's observation long ago that "no object transports us so quickly into pure aesthetic contemplation as the most beautiful human countenance and form" (p. 81). Visual preoccupation is the way attraction is initially expressed. The lover's joy lies in contemplation; it is esthetic appreciation that gives another person's attractiveness its highest value. Curiously, trivial qualities often eclipse great qualities, and one trait may be magnified beyond all others. Grant builds his theory on the contention that the role of facial expression, of the eyes in particular, is emphasized perhaps more than any other factor of attraction in both fictional and factual accounts of romantic fixation.

Thus the many varieties of erotic attraction range between polar opposites. The nearer one's love is to being pure romantic idealization, the more the loved one is experienced in terms of esthetic qualities and the more elevated are one's emotions. Conversely, the nearer one's love is to being pure sexual desire, the less the loved one is experienced in terms of esthetic qualities and the less elevated are one's emotions.

The ideal of married love is the perfect fusion of the esthetic, the sexual, and the practical. It is the practical that stands opposed to the romantic. The different socialization of males and females frequently means a greater difficulty for women to assimilate sex into love and greater difficulty for men to assimilate love into sex. Mature love seeks to fuse the two—the esthetic and the sexual—into one.

Passion Intensified in the Presence of Obstacles

Plato wrote that *eros* (desire) intensifies in the presence of an obstacle. That is, desire is challenged and hence reinforced by obstacles. The romantic ideal of love envisions love overcoming every obstacle that might stand in its way. The strength of true devotion is thought to be greater than the strength of any obstacle. Today obstacles may vary from the ring on the young woman's finger, her indifference to a young man's persistent approaches, to the objections of her parents. It may be the young man's intimation that another is first in his thoughts or his indifference to her approaches. Among those who fall in love later in life, marriage may be the chief obstacle that inflames the passion of a secret love. In our culture an interracial romance faces the very formidable obstacle of social prejudice. Whatever the obstacle happens to be, it often has the effect of stimulating desire.

Anxiety and tension are created by any obstacle to the realization of a desired relationship, and this is sufficient in case after case to excite and challenge the lover and to raise the level of passionate feelings. Years ago the American philosopher William James wrote, "Romeo wants Juliet as the filings want the magnet, and if no obstacle intervenes, he moves toward her by as straight a line as they."[12] This, I'm sure, is true. But what if an obstacle does intervene? Passion rises to the challenge: suspense is a stimulating precondition that never discourages the true romantic, for this is part of the romantic ideal—true love overcomes anything that dares to stand in its way.

There is a frightening aspect to all of this. We know that passion is not rational. In proportion to the strength of the obstacle and the initial desire of the lover, obstructed passion can rise even to the point of violence. In the heat of passion all vestiges of love may disappear. A jealous passion may result in destructive acts, playing out a scenario the very opposite of love. If one cannot gain his or her love, it is better that love be destroyed!

It is passion that causes lovers to feel that love has infused them with a new zest for life, with a mysterious new energy and capability. They attribute this liveliness to love. Unfortunately, such passionate awakening is sometimes taken for quite a different energy—that which is needed to solve problems, to engage in routine work, to raise a family, or just to care consistently for another person through all the exigencies of life.

The Law of Diminishing Returns

We may lament the fact, but romantic passion is subject to the *"law of diminishing returns."* This law states that increasingly greater stimuli are required to reproduce the same effect as previously, and that there is a limit to which stimuli can be intensified. The higher the peaks of intensity, the deeper the possible letdown when the stimuli fails. Such is the law of diminishing returns. It applies to everything that can excite the senses. Romantic love is not exempted.

Whenever passion is fulfilled, it is spent for the present. How well this is expressed in Goethe's *Faust:* "Thus in desire I hasten to enjoyment, and in enjoyment pine to feel desire."[13] What happens to desire when it is fulfilled? For the time it ceases to be desire. Only when the fulfillment has passed can desire exist once again. Thus the paradox of pleasure: Desire is passionate as it anticipates and longs for fulfillment. But fulfillment puts an end to that special passion. One cannot enjoy desire and fulfillment at the same time.

Love passions were not meant to continue on an emotional peak, although such peaks are reached occasionally. Passion remains passion as it rises intermittently. Moments of ecstasy cannot be captured and made permanent states; to attempt to do this is to suffer a series of disappointments. Passion unchecked by reason cannot remain moderate but only becomes more desperate as it becomes clear that it is impossible to cheat time and the eroding effect of repetition.

The Passion unto Death

A curious feature of romantic attachments, which novelists have often portrayed, is the close relation between the passions of love and thoughts of death. Passion, as we've seen, is irrational and all-consuming at times. It can inspire in lovers the willingness to die for the image of the beloved, even when they don't know for sure how they would feel if they had to share their lives. But romantic passion causes a lover to say with all sincerity, "If I can't have you, I don't want to live. You are my whole life; I can't live without you." It is at this point that an individual has virtually lost identity, having so thoroughly assimilated into the identity of the love object. The lover experiences an extreme loss of self.

Recent statistics reveal that, in 1977, 34 percent of all suicides of people under age thirty in Los Angeles County were related to the loss of a loved one, a high percentage of these people having been rejected by some lover. Homicide also correlates frighteningly with the loss of a love.

The passion of love leads, strangely, to a world-deny-

ing, world-defying mentality. It is all part of the irrationality of life when it is in the grip of passion. Lovers in
their privatism fantasize that this world is too poor a stage
for so great a love as theirs. How can the world even understand it let alone make room for it? For some this
means that only in death can a perfect union be found,
which nothing on earth can destroy. This is the theme of
some of the classic romances in literary history.

Although passion may rise to violent force or dominate
an individual with irrational fantasies and desires, this is
usually not the case. Life has a way of exerting compen-
sating forces that are aimed at restoring emotional equilibrium. So excessive love passions are never left standing by
themselves for long. In time they must be integrated with
the more ordinary emotions of daily existence. It is the
discovery of all lovers that only in a casual relationship
can passion be sustained, for then it is born as occasion
demands. In any case, romantic love arouses passions it
cannot sustain, even as it stimulates dreams it cannot fulfill. For everything there is a time and place, and for romantic passion it is all too brief a time, all too elusive a
place.

Gathering the Separate Strands Together

For the sake of understanding the dynamics of romantic
love clearly, I have devoted attention to a number of separate themes—the processes of idealization and projection,
the passion unto death, the intensification of passion in
the presence of an obstacle. Before we go further into the
complex of forces at work in the phenomenon of romantic
love, two classic illustrations might prove helpful.

One of the classic love stories of all time is the old Celtic legend of Tristan and Isolde, perhaps best known by the opera so named by Richard Wagner and considered by many his masterpiece. Tristan, nephew of King Mark of Cornwall, has slain Morold, brother of the king of Ireland, and sent his head to Isolde, daughter of the Irish king, who was engaged to Morold. Tristan's own wound does not heal. Disguised as a minstrel, he goes to Ireland seeking the benefit of Isolde's healing art. She heals him but discovers who he is by matching the splinter found in Morold's skull with the notch in the "minstrel's" sword. In spite of this the two become lovers. Back at the court of King Mark, Tristan sings the praises of Isolde. Much impressed, King Mark orders Tristan to return to Ireland to ask the princess to become queen of Cornwall. Isolde is outraged that her lover should seek her hand for another, but she submits nonetheless.

As the ship is nearing the Cornish shores, Isolde calls upon her servant to prepare a death cup for Tristan to drink. She then drinks half the potion herself, only to discover that her servant has mixed not a death potion but a love potion! The two lovers are unable to resist the magic of the cup and meet secretly while the king is on a hunting party. But one of the king's courtiers betrays them, and at the scene of the discovery he wounds Tristan. Taken to Brittany, Tristan lingers close to death, and his servant sends for Isolde. She arrives only in time to see him die. Isolde learns then that the love potion had been mixed. Conscious only of her lover, Isolde sinks by his body and dies.

Swiss University chaplain Robert Grimm provides a useful commentary:

It was not love, but passion, that bound Tristan and Isolde together. They did not love spontaneously. They were the slaves of a destiny that is symbolized by the love-potion. Consequently for them there was no law, no tradition, no morality. For them, passion transcended good and evil. Passion, in fact, was more inflamed by the obstacles in its path than by the person who was its object. The passion of Tristan would not have existed apart from Mark, Isolde's legitimate husband. It is the social, religious, and moral taboos that create passionate love; and when these do not exist, it becomes necessary to create or revive them! With Mark the king out of the way, Tristan could have married Isolde. But that would have spoiled everything, for him and for us who hear the story! In the process of idealizing the romantic passion, it betrays both the senses and the spirit.

Tristan wants his love to be eternal, so he refused to allow it to carry any imprint of duration or change. He has a presentiment that the duration of time will alter, weaken, or exhaust his romantic passion. This would be intolerable, in deadly conflict with the compulsive need for an absolutely satisfying experience that exists in him (and in all of us). He is afraid of satiety, even of the moment of consummation beyond which there is nothing left. Therefore his passion has a continual need to be revived and renewed by obstacles which prolong it indefinitely and prevent it from being fulfilled, and consequently becoming spent. And when it becomes clear that it is impossible to cheat time, he falls back on his last desperate subterfuge, hoping through death to make his passion eternal.[14]

Perhaps no writer has made more of the significance of passion's dependence upon obstacles than Denis de Rougemont.[15] He contends that passion is not kindled for an object near at hand, easily accessible, morally sanctioned, or even generally tolerated. No passion is conceivable in a world where everything is permitted. For passion always presupposes an obstacle to the lovers' embrace. What does this require, in larger terms? Rougemont replies: "a society fermented by an age-old quarrel between the Sacred, creator of taboos, and the Profane, born of their violation" (p. 42). Tristan and Isolde invited the consequences of a forbidden love that exiled them from the community and consumed without truly uniting them; it is this process that forms the great moments of the myth.

Rougemont concludes that:

> the need for passion, confronting social prohibition, immediately projects its own nostalgia for an infinite desire upon it, even calling this projection *destiny*. This, then, is the dialectic of pure Tristanian passion gathering way: themes of the look, of the storm, and of the sword of chastity between two bodies. When their eyes met, there was then only one certitude between them: that everything was decided and that all prohibitions were now indifferent to them. . . . Each breath published their complicity; defying everyone, they suffered a common need to free themselves at last from the sadness of desire, though suffering it was so sweet that the images of fulfillment had already united them in their imagination" (p. 60).

I suppose nearly everyone is familiar with one version or another of the Don Juan myth. Perhaps the best known is *Don Giovanni*, a romantic work composed by Mozart and considered one of the greatest operas ever written. It tells the adventures of a lover, the nobleman Don Giovanni. The scene is laid in Seville about 1650. The handsome Giovanni has broken the hearts of numerous young women. Only Donna Elvira, whom he has deserted during another elopement, remains true to him. Finally, the lover crowns his misdeeds by mistreating the peasant girl Zerlina. All the angry young women now plan vengeance. In a dual Giovanni had killed Don Pedro, the father of Anna, whose heart he had also broken. Later, during a nightly walk, Giovanni invited the statue of Don Pedro to dinner. The bizarre invitation was followed by a bizarre occurrence. In the final scene, the statue of Don Pedro walks into the room, the floor opens up, and flames from the underworld are seen. Demon hands reach up to drag the evil Giovanni down to his doom. And thus the breaker of hearts meets his appropriate end.

The myth lives because it tells us something about one form of romantic love. Here the critique of Rougemont proves especially helpful. A Don Juan presupposes a society encumbered with rules of behavior that he prefers not just to throw off but to infringe. Don Juan knows only one kind of love, the love that is reduced to the level of seduction, to the success of deceptive maneuvers. With him love is a game resembling the passion for hunting. All is fair in this game; for the seducer it is all a matter of winning. Nothing lies beyond save another conquest. Not that Don Juan is indifferent to the laws of morality. If such laws did not exist, he would invent them in order to violate them; this is essential to the passion that motivates him.

The seducer chooses to love as often as he can, for it is Woman he loves, not a given woman, and in each real woman there is that which wants to be seduced and which can be seduced only once. Such "love" by nature can only be love of the moment, love of the episode. It is the occurrence that makes possible the passion of longing. To be shorn of longing—this is what Don Juan found so intolerable. For him longing could never be converted into relationship, into the gratitude of an intimate communion of spirits.

This, says Rougemont, is why the only Don Juan that conforms to the myth is Mozart's Don Giovanni. Rougemont accepts Kierkegaard's description of Don Juan as a power, not a person—the infinite power of passion that nothing can resist. Kierkegaard says that he can understand the frenzied possessiveness of desire but also the absolute triumph of this desire, a triumph it would be pointless to oppose. If perchance thought lingers over the obstacle, the latter derives its importance from arousing passion rather than from actually opposing it; the pleasure is thereby increased, the victory is certain, and the obstacle only a stimulant. Kierkegaard finds in Don Juan a life thus animated by a powerful and irresistible demonic strain. ("The Musical Erotic," *Either/Or;* cited in Rougemont, p. 115).

Thus the two most compelling myths of love the West has created are in reality two negations of true love in marriage. They tell us, rather, something powerful about the ultimate folly of pursuing a purely romantic love. A succinct note upon which to close is that of Rougemont: "Tristan no longer needs the world—because he loves! While Don Juan, always loved, cannot love in return. Or simply in a few words: Tristan, woeful time, joyous eternity; Don Juan, joyous moments, an eternity of hell" (pp. 142–143).

≈ 4

Destiny or
Disillusionment?

> But love is blind, and lovers cannot see
> The petty follies that themselves commit.
> WILLIAM SHAKESPEARE, *The Merchant of Venice*

*I*F WE take the expression often attributed to French poet Paul Valéry "love . . . that passionate attention," and the Spanish philosopher José Ortega Y Gasset's description of romantic love as "a phenomenon of attention,"[1] we have an accurate account of what romantic love is all about.

The Abnormal Fixation of Attention

At any given time it is natural for our consciousness to focus on some particular object, disregarding other objects, which then remain a mere secondary presence. "What gets our attention," we say, "gets us." Whatever becomes the focus of attention takes on greater reality to our minds, or so it seems. Whenever we give undivided attention to anything, that object gains in significance. When Newton was asked how he discovered his system of understanding the universe, he replied, "By thinking about it day and night." His complete concentration of attention was the key. And so it is with romantic love.

Ortega Y Gasset declared, "I believe that 'falling in love' is . . . an abnormal state of attention which occurs in a normal man."[2] If the person who is the object of such attention knows how to take advantage of this privileged position, and nourishes that attention, an inevitable course follows. Attention becomes captive to one person alone, the enraptured captive being drawn to pursue the object with an ever-increasing passion of desire. In the course of this singular fixation all other eligible objects of attention are increasingly dislodged. Only one attains the advantage, and consciousness endows that one with incomparable vividness.

From this beginning the process of idealizaton takes up, building an image quite beyond reality. The one object of attention has acquired by now such vividness as to never quite vanish from consciousness. The person chosen as the object of concentrated attention becomes a constant presence, as though the whole world focuses upon that loved one. The mental fixation becomes so controlling that the infatuated individual is no longer able to restrain the process. The obsession takes on a momentum of its own, creating its own demands and driven by its own impulses. How easily the flames are fanned! All that's required is the game of alternating encouragement and a deeply solicitous attention one day, followed by disdain or indifference the next, then renewed solicitousness the day after, and so on. The fixation grows in proportion to the tension and uncertainty resulting from constantly upsetting the emotional equilibrium.

Falling in love, as Ortega Y Gasset observes, is truly an

"enchantment." In his words, "In the hermetic enclosure of our attention we are incubating the image of the beloved."[3] No wonder lovers feel that their love cannot be affected by this world. How can it, when they give all their attention to thoughts of one another? Here is a true fragmentation of personality caused by the abnormal attention directed to one object. Does this not also account for the careless abandon with which lovers so often treat the demands of daily existence? The objective observer can only regard such surrender to unreality as a form of madness; the individual, quite literally, is "madly in love."

All this accounts for a young person's sudden personality change—lack of desire to eat, to study, to be truly engaged with daily obligations. Though love songs speak of surrendering to love, lovers are not actually surrendering at all; they are captive to an obsessive fixation of attention from which they cannot extricate themselves.

How easily young people can be deluded! As Pascal is quoted as observing, "The heart has its reasons which the reason knows not of." All good and well, but may this not merely point to the irrationality that accompanies romantic fascination? It recalls C. S. Lewis' comment, "I think you can be madly in love with someone you would be sick of after ten weeks; and I'm pretty sure you can be bound heart and soul to someone about whom you don't at that moment feel excited, any more than you feel about yourself."[4]

As emotion apart from reason, as imagination apart from reality, as an obsessive fixation of attention, this kind of love is singular and all consuming. It is also temporary madness—*eromania*.

The Private World of Love

Romantic lovers tend toward exclusivism and privatism. As a coule they seek some place of their own where a chain of stimulus and response can go on exclusively between them. Secrecy and privacy go together, ideally allowing romantic love to develop, as it were, in a cocoon. To lovers nothing in all the world matters but "our love." In this way a couple naturally builds a sense of their special oneness and a sense of separation from the world. When they have created a world of their own where everything is excluded but their love, life's broader realities become obscured and distorted. The dimensions of living are greatly diminished.

The privatism of romantic love gives us a clue to the lover who says, "Life is like a dream; I'd like to stay right here forever." This is a true perception, for commonly enough lovers withdraw their interest from the world at large for awhile, focusing upon the more vivid reality of a loved one. A person is then enjoying a lyrical state. Even one's closest friends no longer seem necessary to one's well-being or happiness. This is the private world of love.

The psychoanalyst Hubert Benoit commented, "The lover feels buoyant in a world of menace."[5] This is his way of saying that the external world strangely loses its full reality to lovers, even its most urgent and critical concerns. Former preoccupations now cease to be significant at all. This is the passive side of the matter; the active side is the abandon with which lovers throw caution to the winds, as it were, living recklessly as though there were no tomorrow.

To more objective observers cutting off all other inter-

ests and withdrawing from social activities and friendships is opting for a restricted life for which there is a
price to pay. For one thing, it is inevitably to invite the
monotony of a closed-in life. In time the problems relating to such a diminished lifestyle will catch up and cause
no end of trouble, even the possible splitting up of the
once-enraptured pair.

Lovers who cut themselves off from the external world
arrive at last at a point where they have nothing to say to
each other. Communication breaks down on the side of
the essential content needed to inform it. The communion
of two minds dries up for want of renewed nourishment,
which can only come with input from outside themselves.
So eventually a successful couple will have to align their
twosome with other people, groups, interests, and activities. However much they may resist, the practical arrange-
ments of living sooner or later will break into their cozy
situation. Will they then be prepared for this new demand upon them?

As two people become more deeply involved with each
other, a sense of unity develops almost magically. They
begin to reach out subconsciously, seizing upon any evidence that might conceivably confirm their growing assumption that "we're meant for each other." Simulta-
neous responses seem more than coincidental. Looking
intently for symbols of their unity, they find them on every hand "(Hey, they're playing our song!"). Without
their being aware of what is taking place, their separate
individualities are being subordinated to the relationship.
In the process a sense of shared identity is being forged
ever more strongly. A mutuality builds—mutual appreciation, mutual sympathy, mutual concern. Each begins to

feel necessary to the other, and vice versa. Layers of common involvement add daily to a binding sense of "we" and "us." So whether it's a laugh, a tease, or a worry, whatever is shared becomes a subtle but real link in putting together a relationship. But is it love? Romantic passion makes it seem so. And, as Charles Williams reminds us, "A thing that seems has at least the truth of its seeming."[6]

A couple's imagined unity may simply demonstrate a rather basic sociological fact: Our patterned lives elicit standardized responses; that is, two people laugh at the same thing, are moved by the same song, or are attracted to the same groups or interests because they respond to the same cultural cues. It is easy to forget that one reason two people may be held together is because they have been socialized in the same cultural values and tend to respond to the same cultural cues. It is easy not to recognize how many shared experiences are quite universal and how many others are purely coincidental. We make them out to be what we want them to be. Romanticism makes us highly proficient at this.

Any two young people going together may be expected to develop a mutual-support system that increasingly takes over. The process generates its own momentum, creates its own special needs. With it also develops a sense of obligation, because each owes the other more all the time or comes to think so. "Coupleness" is convenient and comfortable. More than that, the couple's social circle, however diminished by romantic privatism, now seems complete with just the two of them. In the process they overlook the fact that any of a number of other partners would be perfectly interchangeable; given the same developing conditions, the same love phenomenon would come about.

The sense of unity increases as romantic love generates its own special language. We need to recognize that language is part of the culture of love; it becomes a special creation of two people, incorporating exclusive symbols meaningful only to them. Their communication system is an esoteric form of special relating. Pet names, inside jokes, idioms, and subtle nuances make the two of them the *insiders*, all others the *outsiders*. They are building their own separate history and culture, surrounding and informing it with sentiments that give psychic reinforcement to the whole love mystique. How strongly the impression is confirmed that their life together is truly one life. But is it the oneness of a true, enduring love?

That romantic love is ardent and intense there can be little doubt. But what guarantee is there of its permanence? Allen Fromme says, "Romantic love is thus a delicious art form but not a durable one."[7] Aaron Rutledge, a well-known marriage counselor and author, finds from his survey of available research that the "I can't live without you" kind of love ends somewhere between six and thirty months after it begins.[8] My own experience would suggest a bit earlier to a bit later.

That romantic love cannot last is one of the disillusionments of the young. The popular writer Lucy Freeman, describing youthful courtship, writes, "They career through courtship, hurtle through the honeymoon, and plunge into the prosaic business of living together. Then, all too often, deep disillusionment destroys the romantic spell and they are left tragically wondering what torpedoed their passionate love."[9]

The youthful myth is that the love they've shared is strong enough to last forever. It has an indestructible quality, so they think. Not that they've witnessed any enduring models of romantic love. But they're sure their love is different from all others. They tell each other so and believe their own declarations. The reality, however, is that those who fall in love sooner or later fall out again. Whether they marry or separate, the romance will end; the only uncertainty is whether it will end abruptly or through a lingering process. But it will end.

Gamesmanship

Romantic love can be described as a game—a seductive, leisure-time, sex-tease game, played for big stakes, the players going for the payoff at the end. As Eric Berne has suggested, the principal function of the preliminary moves is to set up the situation for the payoff. Even the language of courtship is game language: playing the field, playing hard to get, playing for keeps.

Like most games romantic love follows a somewhat mysterious, intriguing course. There are pitfalls, setbacks and recoveries, even second chances along the way. Players are required to have skill and concentration as well as dedication to winning. Because there is rivalry, there must be careful strategy, with each move plotted in advance. In the game of love the possibility exists for winning it all or losing it all. So there must be total commitment, giving it everything one has. After all, this is a fateful adventure, as risky as it is exciting.

We must recognize that some individuals delight in playing the game though they have no intention of winning the prize. As strange as it may seem, it's the fun and excitement of the game itself; their only commitment is to playing. The payoff at the end? That is a trap to avoid. Thus it is that marriage is not always the goal in the game of love. So if marriage is his goal but not hers, then he must guard against giving himself too completely to the game. He must be sure he's not involved with an addicted game player. What's fun for her will be bitterness for him!

Interestingly, romantic love has the advantage of being nurtured in hours of leisure. It entered our culture as a pastime of the leisured classes. So it thrives during relaxed times when spirits are free, unencumbered by responsibilities, problems, or the burdens of school or work. It thrives in those times when there's nothing better to do than play games, explore and stimulate one another, laugh, tease, and just enjoy one another's presence. Much can be made of these playful episodes, these superficial activities where life can be lived in the shallows. No work and all play keeps romantic love alive.

Leisure-time occasions are times when negative moods can be temporarily laid aside or kept relatively hidden. People can wear their best attitudes, be on their best behavior, and play all the right roles—for a time. Ample relief is afforded in the hours two people are not together, when there is time to break away from the game playing, time to lessen the intensity of emotion, time to balance the superficial with more serious pursuits. The beauty of it all is that romantics can live rather easily in their two worlds. Not at all does the leisure world of romance need to conflict with the demanding real world of obligation and responsibility. The two can be kept separate for the most part. And because the leisure hours are very special times, two people can arrange not only what they'll do together but also how they will feel and behave. In such settings they can show each other what is most congenial and interesting, what is freest and gayest about themselves, or at least emphasize that side. They can also arrange the self-image they wish to be most apparent. How very different from the demanding and revealing relationship of marriage!

The Dark Side of Romantic Love

In the course of romantic love one learns that human relationships are not altogether simple and sweet, as they first appear. Quickly enough two people find that there is a problem with managing the ambivalence of human emotions as well as with the conflicts that arise whenever two human beings find themselves in a close relationship.

Ambivalence means that within the same person there are opposing feelings. Ambivalence is illustrated in the episode involving a little girl who had been reprimanded by her mother and went to her room to sulk. She decided to express her feelings by writing her mother a note. This is what it said:

> Dear Mommy,
> I hate you.
>   Love,
>   Nancy

In every relationship along with times of attraction there will be times of aversion; with times of closeness, times of distance; with warmth, coolness; with passionate desire, indifference; with liking, disliking. Mature love can cope with this fluctuation of emotion, because it is founded not solely upon emotion but upon commitment and caring. Not so with romantic love; it succumbs to the stress the negative emotions create, and the lovers easily become anxious if not altogether disenchanted. Similarly, romantic love lacks the resources to cope with conflicts successfully.

Jealousy is a powerful emotion capable of destroying all but the best of loves. It ever lurks nearby, especially solicitous of romantic loves. Jealousy arises out of the fear of losing what one considers his or hers by right of relationship. Jealousy roots firmly in the claims of entitlement that romantic lovers arrogate to themselves—the possessiveness—the prerogative so commonly assumed by lovers.

Fundamentally, jealousy is the ego's reaction in the face of a threatened or real loss of a loved one to someone or something other than oneself. This is easy to understand inasmuch as romantic love is a major prop to self-esteem. The loss, or threat of loss, of a loved one causes the lover to feel rejected, undesirable, perhaps worthless. These feelings are represented in the plea, "But I can't live without you." To the degree that one's identity incorporates that of another person, to the degree that one has assimilated the other into his or her own sense of identity, to that degree the loss of the other is a loss of self. Directed against anyone or anything that threatens to bring about such a loss is the emotion we call jealousy. It is emotion defensive and striking back.

A jealous person is really not jealous of a potential rival so much as jealous of his or her own place, which is why jealousy can direct itself against those who are not really rivals at all. Friends, recreational activities, attention to studies, occupational demands—whatever competes for time and attention—can trigger jealousy. Jealousy can be most irrational, created largely within the jealous person's own anxious ego; whether or not there is a cause is beside the point.

Jealousy is the affliction of people with rather fragile egos, people who in some way have been left out in the past and so have a basic anxiety that this will happen to them again. Suspicion, like fear of rejection, is an ingrained part of their makeup. Jealous people usually have a predisposition toward jealousy.

What becomes so frustrating is that jealous fears are entirely independent of anything anyone can do to alleviate them. Often jealous people will respond to attempts to allay their fears with, "If there weren't something to it, you wouldn't be trying so hard to disprove it." Any new actions at this point seem only to breed new suspicions.

To the degree that one partner feels less in control of the relationship than he wants, to that degree he is susceptible to jealous fears. Perhaps the woman feels she is not desirable enough to hold her man; the man feels he is not manly enough to hold his woman. Because idealized images may be involved, the problem is worsened. Each partner, trying to live up to the other's expecations and idealizations, manages a fairly convincing performance for awhile. But doubts are bound to arise, until soon jealous fears of anyone or anything that exposes the exaggerated, unrealistic image for what it is loom large. A lover who is unable to share the beloved with family or closest friends is a threatened, jealous individual.

Early in the game the jealous party becomes overly possessive, seeking to monopolize the other's time and attention. The jealous person seeks to tighten the relationship, making irrational demands. Before either person knows it, the relationship has become restricting and smothering. The jealous individual is now his own worst enemy, having been made negative and unattractive by his own fears. Nothing is more self-defeating, for the jealous person tends to bring about the very loss that was so greatly feared.

Who can find delight in being with a jealous man or woman? What can more quickly erode the emotions of love? Jealousy causes both parties to make wrong moves. Each tries to anticipate the other—one thinks the worst, then the other overcompensates in the face of a strong reaction. It is a vicious circle, to be sure. The jealousy most likely occurs when the relationship is in its early days, when its tenuousness lends itself to fears. When once those fears become exaggerated in imagination, jealous responses soon follow. Before more solid patterns of mutual affirmation can take root, attention has fixed itself inordinately upon the single concern of "how our love is going." Shallow love leads to jealousy.

If love is real and if adequate time is taken to develop it, a mutual security will eventually supplant all jealous fears. In the meantime, the jealousy-prone partner must seek by all means not to tighten up the relationship. Pressure only makes things worse. There must be every endeavor to build trust, not to indulge the fantasies of mistrust. As we will discuss at length in later chapters, committing the relationship to God can help one remain positive in spirit. And if God is given charge of one's life, he can be trusted to bring out of it a new understanding and new freedom for both parties. The jealous spirit can be healed.

The Fight Against Time

Most important to the final determination of any love is the element of time. In *L'Amour*, Paul Géraldy reflects, "The history of a love affair is the drama of its fight against time."[10] Time is all that is required to scale down idealizations, remove projections, reduce myths to realities, and expose the hard facts of our humaness. It doesn't take long before our faults and failings evidence themselves to the person intimately related to us. And so far as passionate desire is concerned, William Butler Yeats said it exquisitely: "Desire dies because every touch consumes the myth." He means simply that romantic desire first builds upon myth—the creation of novelty and mystery, idealization and projection—but then reality gradually replaces all myths and idealizations—"every touch consumes the myth."

Romantic love is weakened and eventually exhausted by time; time is its nemesis. The initial excitement of fulfilled desire cannot continue endlessly. What once was so new and novel becomes familiar and common; what previously was unknown or only partially known becomes wholly known; the formerly inaccessible is at last possessed in full. There is no longer any reason to contrive romantic surprises or transient thrills. For the lovers who continue to believe that romance should last indefinitely, desire takes the urgency of desperation. It is nothing less than the "knell of fatality"; romantic love cannot cheat time.

All ecstatic excitement—and romantic passion is no exception—stands in frightening contrast to its brevity. The feelings of love may indeed transform our lives for the moment, but a twofold question arises: Can we live for our feelings? or for the moment?

Time inevitably and invariably will disclose the fragility of any romanticized relationship. B. F. Skinner, the noted behaviorist psychologist, has demonstrated that mild positive reinforcement at variable intervals is the best way to sustain passionate desire. This is a possiblity that eludes those who live together. The married no longer meet and love occasionally. They may expect peak experiences from time to time, but they cannot expect to live on peaks continually. Only romanticism dares to presume that such idyllic moments can be anything more than intermittent.

When Romantic Momentum Is Lost

Never is it easy to play idealized roles, to be always humorous, beautiful, charming, good-natured, sympathetic, alert, and so on. When a romance reaches a plateau, then begins to lose momentum, and there follows some deep anxiety that it isn't going anywhere, the usual response is some compulsive action to get it in motion once more. Attempts of this sort may include tightening up the relationship. But is there anything more pathetic than the desperate efforts so often employed to prop up a sagging love affair? Every move on the part of the anxious party to recover the lost passion proves futile. Once the momentum has stopped, the process can begin to reverse itself with incredible speed.

C.S. Lewis caught the pathos of it when he wrote, "Every human love, at its height, has a tendency to claim for itself a divine authority. Its voice tends to sound as if it were the will of God Himself. . . . We may give our human loves the unconditional allegiance which we owe to God. Then they become gods; then they become demons. Then they will destroy us, and also destroy themselves." Or in George Bernard Shaw's words, "When you clasp the idol it turns out to be a rag doll like yourself." So, indeed, what we idolize and clasp tightly to ourselves turns at long last into nothing more than our commonness in pale reflection.

From a slightly different angle, Father Robert Capon writes: "It's the 'You are my destiny' bit. Only God can be that, and any attempt to put so large a demand on a mere creature always comes a cropper. Besides, in marriage it's hard to keep up the appearance of being somebody's destiny." It is expressed more classically in Thackeray's novel *Henry Esmond*. Beatrix says to Henry, "All the time you are worshipping I know very well I am no goddess, and grow weary of the incense." Thus do all our idealized images fade under constant exposure. Each partner sees the basic maneuvers of the other for what they are. No, we cannot forever idolize a beloved; pedestals tend to topple in time.

Although a chosen bondage, romantic love sometimes chafes upon the more independent of the two people involved. It is not at all unusual for one partner to feel pressed into a binding, stifling involvement which he or she comes to resist and may eventually even come to hate because it limits independence. Whereas in a more mature love there is both a binding quality and a releasing quality, in romantic attachments there is little sense that the relationship releases one to develop one's individuality. Not infrequently it is this sense of being bound that leads to the breakup of two people who so shortly before wanted nothing more than to be together always.

Whatever the changing conditions that bring about a breakup, and when it is perceived that a relationship isn't going to last, the strength of the initial expectations transfers into equally devastating feelings of rejection, especially for the partner who isn't willing to relinquish the relationship. But devastating loss is not the only feeling to accompany the ending of a love. When a lover who drops out seems almost to hate the other partner, how are such feelings explained? It may well be that they are really misdirected emotions that originate in self-disgust for having overvalued and overcommitted oneself to an idealized person. Because of self-pride these feelings are directed against the former loved one, who becomes the scapegoat. It is likely that one would rarely be aware of doing this, perhaps recoiling at the very suggestion.

In other words, because romantic passions are often dramatic and overpowering, so, too, the final disillusionment takes on a similarly dramatic force. Young people normally quite genial and not given to extreme emotional reactions are shocked to find how intense their feelings of resentment and bitterness become once they've turned from the person who so recently had them enthralled. This radical turnabout is encountered frequently in student counseling.

It is interesting to note that most contemporary love songs deal with the anxious, painful aspects of love, the pleadings and partings, the passionate but unfulfilled longings, and the bitterness of breaking up and looking back. Some 70 percent foster an attitude of caution and mistrust in a love that is unpredictable and highly changeable, given to violent mood swings. Paradoxically, it is desperately difficult to live *with* such love, or to live *without* it. Rarely do these songs extol the qualities of commitment beyond disappointment or of caring for the deeper needs of the total individual.

When misunderstanding, doubt, or conflict lead lovers to even a temporary separation, feelings can be just as devastating. The sense of loss is comparable, and there is the added agony of suspense; the outcome is still unresolved. Why, though, should the feelings of loss be equally intense? We need to understand more adequately than we do that the loss or threatened loss of a person is, in its most profound sense, the loss of one's own newly acquired self, one's real identity. The trauma, the disorientation, the despair all reflect the loss of self.

Whenever this kind of self-loss occurs, the exciting lover who existed briefly is gone; the individual feels once again the colorless, uncertain, longing-filled person he or she has always been. At least in part the broken heart is the direct result of a shattered self-image, which had shone brightly though briefly during the height of the attachment.

As surely as the tides, lovers are forced in time to recognize that the object of romantic desire does not match in reality the person so perfectly constructed in the wishfulness of the heart. She has faults, loses her temper, is obstinate, has moody days. He is not always concerned to be immaculately groomed, is grumpy and out of sorts when things do not go his way, and spends money carelessly. Their love, so exquisite and all-embracing in romantic hours, is somehow unable to cope with these disappointments. The question, sadly, can be asked, "Have we been duped by love's illusions?"

The Spanish philosopher Miguel de Unamuno reflected on the brief course of this form of love: "Love is the child of illusion and the parent of disillusion." The force of reality sooner or later brings down every glorious illusion that romance created. Where lovers first saw themselves as different from the rest of the species, before long they regain their identity with humanity, once again act like their everyday selves. Love like this must turn the corner, must shed its myths and illusions, so as to begin the developmental task of building upon a foundation of reality and reason. Should it fail in this, such love will self-destruct.

It Can Happen at Fifty

Most analysts regard the love we've been examining as fundamentally an adolescent phenomenon, a developmental stage in emotional and social growth for young people. When it occurs among "middlescents"—people in their middle years—it represents a regression, a return to an unfulfilled earlier stage. Many an older man today leaves his wife for a younger woman, falling in love all over again, often claiming it as the first time ever. It is not unusual for him to say, "I've never felt this way before. I've never known such power of love! She's given me a zest for living and an appreciation for things I've never even noticed before." How do we account for this? Are the same dynamics at work that lead adolescents into romantic loves? The answer is a resounding *yes!*

Many of these men know full well that they are succumbing to an illusion that can only disrupt life and eventually destroy two people, perhaps even two whole families. Why do they walk into what they know to be a trap, an emotional, romantic trap? Why do they allow passion and ego-needs to suddenly take control? Why are they willing to risk so much? To throw over the wisdom that experience has taught them for years? Can this be love?

After years of counseling those involved in extramarital love affairs, I'm persuaded that many men and women find themselves in a grip of passion, with which reason cannot compete. Still others do not understand what's happening to them, locating the cause outside themselves. Of course, any romantic involvement is an exciting, pleasurable interlude in a life grown dull and monotonous with routine and familiarity. Perhaps there has been a failure to find success and adequate rewards in one's career. Perhaps there are fewer rewards in marriage—the marriage one has long since ceased nurturing. The affair is a tempting compensation for the love that's lost its luster. Perhaps a man doesn't recognize a compelling need to restore a slipping self-image and the temptation to satisfy that need through the flattering attention of a younger woman—a woman who at the time may be tempted to participate in a romantically stellar performance involving herself and an admired man. They share a make-believe world.

"You really understand me," he purrs into her ear as they dine in the seclusion and dim lights of some posh restaurant. "You always bring out the best in me. I feel alive again when we're together; you're magic to my spirit! I've never felt so close to anyone before!" And so it goes. What he really means, if he could honestly face his own motives, is that he's relieved to get away from the one person—his wife—who completely understands him, who is no longer enamoured with what she knows, and whose true perceptions keep him from flights of fancy. What he wants, what he needs, is the affirmation of an attractive woman who doesn't know him intimately, a woman he can impress, who momentarily at least is caught up with the idealized image he is acting out. He is hoping he might discover himself to be the man he's always wished, the man he's confident he can be. All he needs is a little first-class encouragement, and this he subconsciously arranges for himself through the means of the younger woman.

She may be coming from a completely different set of circumstances and may have entirely different needs. Yet the attention she receives may find a response within her that is both alarming and confusing. Perhaps a meaningful relationship has recently ended, leaving her with a sense of loneliness, perhaps rejection. To be affirmed once again makes it dangerously easy to overlook the complicating circumstances.

The affair may be a welcome diversion, a momentary tranquilizing of a burdensome, anxious situation either in his career or at home. Here's a nice break from hard reality. After all the tough years of keeping his nose to the grindstone—and for what?—isn't it time for a little reward in terms of romantic affirmation? Subconsciously, too, it may be the rather compelling need of the middle years to prove one's attractiveness at a time when confirmation from other quarters has largely dried up. Soon it will be too late; it is now or never!

What comes into such a man's life as a fresh, new event is bound to be stimulating, especially when it is secretive and furtive, risky enough to confirm his boldness and daring. There is a curious new freedom he's experiencing, perfectly understandable inasmuch as there is no past as yet to regret, no future as yet to dread, and no present sufficiently established to doubt. For the time being at least there exists no need, as in marriage, to work out compromises between opposing sets of interests. The reawakening of passion seems all but beyond belief, while the new zest for living is ample proof that the capacities of one's youth have only lain dormant, waiting for the person who could waken them to life. Playing the new role recaptures the features of a former youthfulness. "Look at me! I'm a pretty good lover after all! There's a lot of life left in the old boy yet!" He also discovers another ability that he would hardly attempt to demonstrate at home—flirtation. No wonder he's excited, suddenly having all those long-buried talents released—nothing so appealing and challenging has happened in years. A new business venture is dull by comparison. What further justification is needed beside the reawakening of love that is taking place?

Now, of course, this is a most pitiable condition. Deception is paramount. To our momentarily reinvigorated friends it seems there is no tomorrow—no price to pay; but there is. To temporarily ignore this fact is to succumb to a will-o-the-wisp. The new affection is likely no more than a regressive need for self-affirmation. For two people at the same place and the same time the situation was ripe for a romantic adventure.

The scenario is easily contrived. The woman passes by and smiles, an invitation in her eyes. His returning smile betrays a ready response. As yet there is nothing extraordinary about what has taken place. But an excitation has occurred on the periphery of both their sensibilities. Swiftly an ego-message leaps to his mind: "I'll bet I could attract her to me without half trying." Suddenly need and imagination are fused together. All remembrance of his married status, all thought of their difference in age and placement in life—everything of significance to real life is obscured by the excitement and the fantasies in his mind. An amazing change is taking place, as though irresistible forces are at work.

Two vulnerable people have begun to interact in what appears to be a casual manner, yet it is weighted with profound meanings. The young woman, possibly his professional colleague, happens to be in a down mood. He detects it immediately. She could use a boost in morale about now, he reasons quite correctly. And she? Little had she realized that such an empathic, willing counselor was nearby, someone who was more than glad to have her turn to him. In his own need he welcomes the role of indispensable friend and counselor. How natural to build upon the already established base of understanding between them. In his desire for understanding and a smooth relationship he may forget that her occupation depends upon her professional ability to serve; her very livelihood may rest upon her talent for anticipating needs for which he shares responsibility. Her professionalism demands that she be properly groomed, efficient, positive in spirit, responsive. As she serves their common professional interests, she serves her own chances for promotion and recognition. But in the blur of life's complexities and in the ambiguity of personal responses to one another, it isn't difficult to misread each other's intentions. To two people with deep needs the developing situation may appear to represent the beginning of a meant-to-be love. Every action that follows supports this notion. The trap is set!

Depending on the degree of dissatisfaction a person may be experiencing at home, and whether one regards it with hopefulness or not, the new excitement produces a first move in the other's direction. That first move is psychological, a move in imagination only. It emerges from the periphery where it first received the stimulus—of course, without conscious, present participation in the process. In its beginnings this represents only an almost instinctive response of men and women to each other. It is a daily occurrence for many. Usually such attraction is not followed by any overt action. Innumerable attractions of this kind are erased from thought almost as soon as they occur. But if one is predisposed by some felt need, that first move may then turn into an overt pursuit of the love possibility. And it may get set in motion before two needy individuals are aware of what is happening.

Tragically, most people are caught in such situations without recognizing the dynamics prompting them. Often they contend with great seriousness that this is the first time they've felt "real love." Yet, however perceived or rationalized, this love is actually the creation of an idealized relationship, coming straight out of imagination and urged on by one's present need for self-affirmation. However, there is a sense in which people fall in love because they want to, although desire may lie outside their conscious awareness. But at some point along the way each individual is fully aware of what's happening and how he or she urges it on, creating the conditions for its continuance. From that point on each one bears responsibility for the developing interaction. For the Christian it is quite inconceivable that the Spirit of God would not bring a clear awareness early in the course of things. Each individual is responsible nonetheless.

The Positive Values of Romantic Love

It might be cause for wonder at this point whether I am intent upon denigrating romantic love altogether, banishing it from life wherever possible. Not so. Despite the analysis of its sometimes deceptive, inadequate ways, it has an established place in the building of positive love relationships. Not that it is indispensable, or present in all instances. But in our culture more often than not romantic love is the prelude to a more mature, truly caring love relationship. It may well serve as the precondition to the love of a fine marriage—that is, if it stabilizes and deepens, cools its passionate fervor, moves away from pure idealizations to more realistic perceptions, and stops playing games. Contained within romantic love are many higher possibilities.

In our culture romantic love is a normal, natural, delightful preoccupation of young people. It is a uniquely valued pleasure, a perfectly healthy part of adolescent growth when it can avoid excesses and in due time is outgrown. No one questions the fact that it is an incomparable experience in the realm of social and emotional life.

Romantic love can lead straight to the choice of a life mate. With that choice is provided a strong emotional reinforcement. As Gail Sheehy says in *Passages*, "The illusions of the twenties, however, may be essential to infuse our first commitments with excitement and intensity, and to sustain us in those commitments long enough to gain us some experience in living."[13]

An intense emotional component is necessary if a person is to choose one from among many. If nothing else, the emotional focus and intensity is a kind of confirmation. Being in love is a way of convincing oneself and others that the choice is indeed a correct one, even when two people feel some qualms about it. By lovers' fixing upon each other's special qualities, whether real or perceived, the value of individuality is accentuated and made central to the selection process. Moreover, the choice can then be viewed as something more than rational; the whole personality is involved, the rational and the emotional.

In many instances romantic love is sufficient to sustain and protect the tenuous early life of a relationship, giving it a chance to grow into something more substantial. And however laden with ego problems, romantic love does teach what it is to care for another person, to give oneself for the sake of another. Here, for the first time, many a young person learns that in order to receive one must give, to receive love one must love. And it might be noted that romantic desire has helped many young people break down their inhibitions, especially those that have kept them from being able to express affection and to verbalize their feelings.

Should a couple marry, only to have doubts encumber their relationship later on, it is a positive thing to be able to look back and say, "Yes, we were deeply in love; we experienced all the wild passions of desire. We know what it is to have reached the peaks of romantic emotion." Were it otherwise, the couple might think themselves cheated, deprived of all that love is said to offer.

As all couples will bear witness, marriage brings difficult adjustments for the most compatible pair. Problem-solving techniques become crucial. Decision making must incorporate the tastes and desires of very different people. All the idiosyncrasies of two individuals must be managed in the partnership. It helps to successfully negotiate the problems of early months if a strong remaining romantic affirmation undergirds the relationship. Romantic emotion supplies the needed incentives to keep working at the adjustments with strong hopefulness, helps make it all seem worth the effort—so needful until other incentives become a part of the process. Without the romantic aspect, the commitment to an enduring marriage might be tenuous and uncertain.

In the process of scaling down idealizations, reducing illusions to realities, and moving toward greater self-disclosure, the faults and imperfections of two people do rise to the surface. If, as we've seen, romantic passion tends to blind one partner to the other's faults, is this all bad? In all likelihood, no. Within the more secure, settled relationship, there can be a gradual coming to terms with these faults as they are disclosed and so the gaining of a gradual ability to manage them. To have them all unveiled at once would be too much for probably the finest developing love.

Long after the romantic peak has receded and its purpose served, a couple can retain this aspect as a powerful memory of their commitment to each other. The sweet nostalgia has a continuing role. The romance of the receding past seems always remembered in its best light, a symbol of all the good things that brought them together and sealed their decision. So when they've experienced all that earlier romanticism could offer, both good and bad, the pair can point to the deeper love that now supersedes that previous version, seeing clearly the depth to which love has grown. To be sure, the new love will be less dramatic but so much more stable and satisfying in the long run.

Very few decisions today are intended as lifetime ones. Where we live and where we work are no longer seen in these terms at all. Marriage is about the only remaining commitment of this kind. But with little future predictability and with increasing numbers of divorces, it takes a lot of faith to say, "until death do us part." To complicate it further, there is less parental guidance than in the past, so the entire weight of decision rests upon the young couple. What seems to assure them that they are right in their decision is the intensity of their love, what we've seen to be the romantic undergirding. Being in love is thus a preliminary stage, neither all good nor all bad, but in most instances probably relatively necessary to the flowering of that which then can mature in its time.

Is There a Christian View?

We cannot say that there is a Christian view of romantic love; at best, we can say that there is a Christian response. Christians should be informed and aware, able to intelligently and prayerfully assess the forces at work in their lives. We must recognize our tendency to act according to self-seeking ways, to accept unrealistic desires and inappropriate passions without checking them against our commitment to God's will. Our responsibility is to seek God's help in order to arrest this process. We must be quick to perceive the social and spiritual consequences of our thoughts, desires, and actions. We must commit our fantasies to the Lord for his review, for his commendation or censure. We must be honest before him about what is going on in our love life and what we truly see our motivations to be. This means seeking to maintain our primary relationship with him. Then we can be confident of his guidance in all subsequent relationships.

There is a Christian dimension to love that transforms every aspect of human loving. Christ's love does not replace, but redeems and transfigures our other loves. Jesus is both the model and the source. We shall direct our attention in later chapters to the possibility of our appropriating the love of Christ. But next we must examine the reasons some individuals have a capacity to love while others do not. What can we expect in terms of correcting any existing deficiency in the capacity to love? The next two chapters are designed to provide some directions in dealing with these questions.

PART II

Caring Love:
The Growing Bond

Loving Is
Something We Learn

Love is possible only if two persons communicate
with each other from the center of their existence.

ERICH FROMM, *The Art of Loving*

ONE OF the truly helpful books on loving is Allan
Fromme's *The Ability to Love*[1] (not to be confused with an
equally outstanding book by Erich Fromm, *The Art of Loving*). Basic to Allan Fromme's thought is the concept that
loving is something we learn. Loving is something we
may learn exceedingly well, or poorly, or not at all. We
are not born with the ability to love, only with the capacity to learn loving. We may, in fact, learn nonloving just
as well. Our ability in later years to love and receive love
depends on our early experiences of learning love or nonlove. Let's look at the negative side first.

Learning the Negatives of Love

There are times in a child's life when his parents are
not very loving, and this leaves a strong imprint. He notices these models of loving and nonloving. The child's

critical first experiences come when his parents make the first demands upon him. Unmixed parental adoration suddenly takes on an entirely new dimension; they want the child to do what they expect not what he wants. He is now expected to feed himself and not to throw his food. He is to smile for people and not get into things. If he expresses his dislike by throwing a temper tantrum, he experiences an especially strong kind of nonlove in return. He feels, with some justification in fact, that his parents do not love him. When they impose their wants on him, deprive him of things he wants, fail to pay attention to him, their actions challenge his developing will to respond in kind. Because he is not able to understand rationally as yet, he can only respond with behavior—*and it is nonlove for nonlove.*

A further lesson in nonlove is learned when a child first encounters a rival, a sibling or someone else. Now he experiences opposition and competition. Learning to defend himself and to fight for his rights is not the same thing as loving. To get ahead means to be aggressive, to beat out someone else, to take or sometimes take back. Patterns of nonloving are learned, sometimes sooner and more thoroughly than patterns of loving.

Among the more subtle and pervasive elements in nonloving is the sense some people develop of unworthiness and guilt. Childhood experience accounts for this, too. Parents, consciously or unconsciously, deliberately or not, reject a child in one way or another in certain situations. They're too busy, too tired, too frustrated, or perhaps just now being pushed beyond their patience. Who gets the backlash? Those nearest to them are most likely to be special targets. Parents project their own unresolved problems, dissatisfactions, hurts, and tensions. As we say, they scapegoat their negative feelings upon their children. These feelings may be expressed as disapproval (with or without declared grounds) or as outright rejection; they may be accompanied by anger or disgust. The child is made to feel unworthy of love, or at best that love is conditional. He can often earn it—if he's good.

All through life an individual may carry a self-image of having been loved or not loved. Later he may enter into a relationship thinking that love will be his only if he earns or deserves it somehow. Love is seen as a reward gained in some kind of exchange system. To be loved for oneself is something he may never expect. And the love he has never received is precisely the love he is unable to give. He is a love cripple.

Of the more damaging things a child learns, certainly one of them is the unreliability of love. Soon enough a child discovers that love is given or withheld unpredictably. Sometimes when he asks, he is given what he asks for; at other times he is refused. Sometimes when he cries he is caressed and comforted; at other times he is ignored, or, worse, somebody screams at him. When he performs well at the table, people may smile; at other times they frown. How can he possibly know that sometimes they are responding not to his performance but to their own headaches and problems? What he has is an impression that love is the most unpredictable, unreliable thing in his little universe.

One myth of romantic love is that it is different; it is utterly reliable—you can count on it forever. Young people in love believe this because they need and want to believe it. They yearn for proof that somewhere in their world such love exists. In this way they are manifesting a need that all human beings have. How very much they want to believe that the one who promises them undying love is going to produce it! For one thing, the promise of love brings assurance of being a person worthy of love after all. Why, here is someone who thinks I'm the most worthy person on earth! This must be right, of course, because look at the emotion that backs it up! This is real love—devoted, utterly reliable, and unconditional.

For lovers so deeply assured by the myth, the promise of love remains intact; that is, until some minor, unexpected thing happens. He forgets the date he made just two days ago or is an hour late because, as he says, he started working on his car and felt like getting the job done before cleaning up. Or perhaps, as a new bride, she has prepared a very special supper as a surprise, only to have her announcement that it's ready bring the response that he'd like to wait half an hour because the last quarter of the game is on television. That's all it takes to bring back the message of childhood—love is unreliable after all. Love isn't what it promises to be; it's a con game!

Let's follow the illustration of the young bride and groom. She falls into a depression, into silence and brooding. Eventually he notices and asks her what is wrong. Her resentment flares because, "You ought to know full well what the trouble is!" So she flatly accuses him of not loving her. He is utterly baffled, hurt by a remark he doesn't understand, and responds defensively, "Of course I love you! What's eating you anyway?" That does it. "See, you even raise your voice at me! What kind of love is that? And besides, nothing is eating me!" So the argument is launched as to whether he loves her or not.

She might well have managed the disappointment, even disguised the hurt, except for one thing: She has been touched at a place made tender at childhood. It's the old, nagging question of whether or not love can be counted on. What is love anyway?

Look at the young husband in the illustration. The marital problem is compounded if he brings into the marriage a similar childhood problem. Suppose his parents were indulgent of his desires to the point of not prodding him to do certain things on time. As the common saying goes, "he got away with murder." Now he's married to a woman used to a tighter scheduling of time, but his request to watch television when he knows supper is on the table doesn't seem to him critical enough to bring her response of anger. Each may seem to overreact when in fact each is simply manifesting a patterned response.

Author David Jones illustrates our point aptly with a personal story: "Love for another person involves demands. My five-year-old son loves his teddy bear but I am not always so sure he loves me, at least not in the same way. His teddy bear never complains, is always there when needed, can be left alone for hours or days at a time and not get angry or huffy. His teddy bear places no demands on him, but his father does. His father's love costs him more."[2]

There is nothing quite like marriage to reveal the vast difference between romantic love and the love that can endure through every hard circumstance. Love is a lifetime venture, and this soon becomes clear. Time fortifies true love, expanding its dimensions and diminishing its illusions. It takes time for the integrating process of love to take place, even for two people to know just what differences between them need integration. Love is made up of compromises, relinquishments, accommodations, apologies, renewals—all kinds of major and minor adjustments. The ambivalence of emotions discussed in Chapter 4 can be managed by the love that commits itself to caring; this, too, takes time and patience, for it is a learning process. Hard work alone is capable of achieving it. Fromme is correct; loving is a learning process. And perhaps nowhere is this fact summarized more succinctly than in the words of author-counselor Walter Trobisch:

> Love is a feeling to be learned. It is tension and fulfillment. It is deep longing and hostility. It is gladness and it is pain. There is not one without the other. Happiness is only a part of love. Suffering belongs to love also. This is the mystery of love, its beauty and its burden. Suffering makes immature love resign or grow into mature love. Immature love cannot endure tension, and it has no patience with anything that stands in its way. It demands and consumes and tries to dominate. Love is a feeling to be learned.[3]

From Romantic Love to Mature Love

Recall for a moment our discussion of romantic privatism, the romantic involvement that draws young people out of the group scene of the youth culture into a closed world for two. Even friendships of long standing suddenly seem superfluous for a period stretching into early marriage. Two lovers continue for awhile to exist only for each other. Even when they are not together they remain inaccessible to other people. This privatism tends to become habit forming. What happens to impede this closing-in upon each other?

Marriage is meant to be the means by which couples are drawn back into the social world. The wedding serves as the ritual of return, reestablishing links of reciprocal obligation between bride and groom and their family and friends. Then, more and more, the outside world reaches in. The private enclosure of "just we two" begins to peel and crack. Despite any and all pretensions to a consuming love, each partner now must settle into purposes and directions other than merely being a love partner. It is in marriage that there is the emergence of the social creature who is, first, part of a pair but also part of a community. Married love finds itself at cross-purposes with romantic love and its ideal of "just we two." As the writer V.A. Demant reminds us, "Lovers meet each other as lovers; now they have to meet as total human beings."[4] Lovers cannot forever remain outside the larger community.

Romantic love diminishes as mature, caring love expands to take its place. For many couples this is not a dramatic change but a transition so smooth as to be imperceptible. Two people simply emerge from their private cocoon, as it were, into the sunlight of a new life together. Now they understand the darkness and restrictedness of the cocoon of their former privatism. The wider world of social love is so much more challenging and rewarding. If they could, would they choose to return to the cocoon? Never! It was secure and warm and perfectly adequate while it lasted. Now there are, by contrast, enormous new demands, problems, even potential for hurts in this social world of married love. But the deepening dialogue of caring love is adequate in a way that cocoon love could never be.

Couples who deeply love do not need to continually go off by themselves but share friendships and take on challenging tasks together. They're no longer preoccupied with their feelings for each other but now are free to turn their attention outward, sharing values and experiences, all of which they find outside themselves. They love with their minds and wills as well as with their hearts and emotions.

What does the will have to do with love? The will has everything to do with love—not the romanticized version but genuine love. That any true love involves intention is brought out by Jesus in his command to love. One cannot respond to a command with emotions, only with intention, with will. A good adage for young marrieds is, "You chose your love; now love your choice." This implies the exercise of the will and is the essence of commitment.

Rollo May has written in *Love and Will,* "Will without love becomes manipulation; love without will becomes sentimentality."[5] He goes on to say that it is our task in marriage to unite love and will; this uniting must become part of our development as a pair. To the extent that this is done it is an achievement that points toward maturity, integration, and wholeness.

Most modern theologians have emphasized this point. Karl Barth has commented, "In contradistinction to mere affection, love may be recognized by the fact that it is determined, and indeed determined upon the life-partnership of marriage. . . . Love does not fall into raptures; it is ready to undertake responsibilities. . . . Love is not only affinity and attraction; it is union."[6]

Genuine love is enduring for the simple reason that it is an act of the will, one person committed to another both intensively and extensively. It never begins with the question of whether or not there shall be a failure later on;

what matters is that marriage is founded on a genuine intention of the will, a commitment to the person and not to one's own feelings or gratifications. Surely this is what the English philosopher John Macmurray had in mind when he said, "Love is the capacity for self-transcendence, the capacity to care for another."[7] Later we shall turn our attention to the power that is singularly adequate to inform the will for its task. Suffice it here simply to say that what God commands, he also enables. His *agape* love, as we will see, is the answer to human inadequacy.

As we move in the direction of clarifying the differences between romantic love and love for life partnership, an abbreviated but helpful distinction is this: Romantic love is characterized by the two big Es—*Ego* and *Emotion;* caring love is characterized by the two big Rs—*Reality* and *Reason.* This formula, of course, isn't all-encompassing, but it is basic; it provides the right clues.

We've seen how romantic love is largely two people massaging each other's egos. Mature love, by contrast, adopts a different objective, a different direction; mature love looks away from self in its concern for the other. The interaction is that of mutual esteem. An essential part of love's definition is this: *Love is that relationship between two people which is most conducive to the optimal development of both.* Another definition of love, often attributed to psychologist Harry Stack Sullivan, is that *love is that condition in which the happiness and well-being of another person is essential to my own.* Romantic love, quite clearly, cannot rise to this height; turned inward instead, its own happiness is the central factor. Mature love is wanting the best for your partner and being willing and glad to pay whatever price is involved. Allan Fromme describes mature love as the total bonding of two people in all their dimensions. This means incorporating love into one's life rather than treating it as some compelling but unrealistic excursion from life. Such developed love abandons all pretense and role playing; it seeks to be as game-free as possible, as open and self-disclosing as possible. It allows for the full expression of mutual trust and respect in order that both parties may maximize their full potential as unique individuals. It is life lived *with* and *for* the other.

The Impossible Dream

Young lovers expect the impossible, that somehow they can have their cake and eat it too, that their marriage will be different from all others they have known. Although others have failed, they expect to maintain an intensely passionate, even breathtaking, love affair, yet at the same time share a calm, stable, and settled existence. The two states are not compatible; this is the hard lesson ahead. And because happiness has been the goal of their initial relationship, they want it to be the goal of marriage also. But, again, happiness is far too restricted a goal for marriage. Love in marriage must relate to all the varied objectives two people share in their partnership, and of these happiness is far from being the most important. At best, happiness comes as a by-product of other achievements, principally that of satisfying work, of homebuilding, and of taking a responsible place in the community, all of which demand a different kind of commitment—a commitment to an unforeseeable future that the two shall share, come what may.

Theodor Reik talks of a new kind of companionship,

quite different from romance but no less valuable, in which idealization has ceased and passion subsides: "The lover has changed into a friend. There is no longer the violence of love, but the peacefulness of tender attachment."[8] It recalls the words of C.S. Lewis: "Lovers are always talking to one another about their love; friends hardly ever about friendship."[9] The couple's preoccupation is no longer just with each other but with the goals and challenges life has put before them.

Allan Fromme notes that husbands and wives who have progressed to a settled, mature love can look back and feel that they now have something that their earlier love had presumed but not actually included. They appreciate the memories of their early love but feel little need to return to it. They have so much more now that, in retrospect, they feel as though they were relative strangers then. Now they find their love in many facets of their life together rather than in the few with which they started and upon which they had pinned so much. It is indeed a very different love. Life in partnership is lived according to very ordinary emotions, and this is possible only after the emotional momentum of passionate love has subsided. Because of its dramatics, its heroics, and its excesses, romantic passion can sometimes give the impression of greater devotion than does the deepest mature love. But this is sheer illusion, as every mature couple knows so well. Love becomes part of our way of life rather than a mere set of feelings we only occasionally and extravagantly express. Love in marriage rises or falls with our ability to meet the daily problems of living together. In the long run our love cannot exceed our ability to get along with the person to whom we were initially attracted.

Journalist Ernest Havemann has reflected on this, reminding us that there comes a day when we have to admit that being in love and being married haven't changed us after all.[10] We are just as ordinary, have the same limitations, faults as well as virtues, and we can be cranky just as we can be tender. Sometimes we are carefree but other times beset with worries. We are, in other words, still human stuff, and so is the husband or wife we've acquired. We do not feel totally unselfish even toward our wives or husbands. Besides our love we also have strong feelings of rivalry, and dislike for them at times. We haven't shed our ability to be absentminded, foolish, irrational and prejudiced, lazy, or—and you can add a dozen or more disabilities to the list.

Because all of this is part of the hazard of being human—equally true of Christians as of non-Christians—we need other resources adequate to satisfy quite different needs than those met by romantic courtship—needs for mutuality of purpose, for sustained companionship through life's disappointing and bleak times. These needs require an extensive rather than an intensive love, one with staying power not stimulating power. This means a commitment to caring not a commitment to happiness.

All human love is inherently tragic, and we must accept this fact. The British theologian Sherwin Bailey makes this point, showing that love is always the conjunction of two free, autonomous people, and the consequent clash of two wills to power.[11] Nicholas Berdyaev wrote that "pure tragedy arises when . . . a conflict of values takes place between the value of love and the value of freedom."[12] Each partner challenges the other's freedom as it has never been challenged before. It is the work of love to mitigate, even to transform this conflict. Only love can do it.

The tragedy of love consists in its being subject not only to conflict of interests or the clash of two wills to power but to our sinful impulses and hence to the possibility of betrayal. Because love is an inward condition, it is subject to the secrets of inward betrayals, inward infidelities—unfaithfulness that may never manifest itself outwardly and hence may be obscured even from the awareness of the individual whose problem it is. Inward betrayals are no less damaging than outward.

How important it becomes to keep one's spirit open to the revealing, convicting Spirit of God, in order that all waywardness of heart be honestly confronted. The subtleties of sin work most insidiously when the tempting justification for an unfaithful heart appears in the guise of love for someone else. Boston University professor Peter Bertocci makes the point when he says that "the love of two persons is no stronger than their values, and marriage will be a crucible within which these values will be tested."[13] Within marriage we elaborate precisely those values that are most meaningful to us, whether they have been previously in play in our lives or suppressed. Our true values invariably surface within the ongoing rituals and routines of daily life, and especially when life's very real demands militate against romantic sentiments of any kind. Then we need "tough love," nothing less.

Incidentally, we are mistaken if we think that sexual fidelity is a correlate of mature love. It is a consequence not of moral restraint but rather of the satisfactions and values two partners deem most important to marriage. Sexual fidelity is a means of serving one another while at the same time preserving the higher objectives of marriage. The joys and rewards of a loving, faithful life partnership mean more than any transient, merely sensual gratification of the present.

In earlier chapters considerable space was devoted to the relation between self-worth and the need for love. We should look at it briefly once again, this time from a more advanced perspective.

The greater our sense of self-worth and the more confident we are about our place in relation to our loved one, the less easily we are hurt by any actions we might be tempted to interpret as the erosion of love. It is when our sense of self-worth becomes excessively dependent on receiving love from our mate that the entire relationship gets into trouble. When married people feel sure of themselves as individuals, this reflects itself in open, relaxed reaching out to one another. Then it is possible to be self-disclosing without feeling threatened and to have an open relationship impervious to all the forces that could sink a less secure marriage.

Psychologist Herbert Otto, in *Love Today*, contends that love makes us feel more worthy as individuals but that this is more properly a by-product of love than its main product. He says, "Love can and does give us greater self-esteem, but this is part of the process of love, not *the* process."[14]

A crucial element in any definition of love appears to be this: *Love is the creative interaction of two mature individuals whose relationship is based on mutual esteem.* But only as both parties have a strong, stable sense of their own self-worth is mutual esteem possible.

Erich Fromm distinguishes infantile love as "I love because I am loved"; whereas mature love is "I am loved because I love." Immature love says, "I love you because I need you"; mature love says, "I need you because I love you." A world of difference separates the two.[15]

To whom is love more important—husband or wife? Until recently, the apparent answer would be the wife. In support, some might quote Lord Byron: "Man's love is of man's life a thing apart. 'Tis woman's whole existence." But in Byron's time, the beginning of the nineteenth century, woman was hardly yet emerging as a person autonomous and free in her own individuality. Then, and for so long a period of human history, it was "man's world, woman's place." Modern conditions have changed this, so that both men and women are adopting new roles, and necessarily so. Women have become men's companions and equals in every respect. Thus both sides of Byron's equation are pretty thoroughly modified today. No longer is a woman's love the whole of her existence, and a man's love is becoming far more deeply integrated into his whole life. In other words, love today involves the interaction of whole people in every dimension of the marital partnership. Love means desire for a *whole* person and a *real* person. No longer does love abstract certain features or isolate certain expressions and activities from the more comprehensive personal context. Love is an all-embracing, total engagement of two people with each other.

The somewhat harried woman on the television talk show was not altogether amiss when she said, "Love is all the stuff we've been through together." She referred to love as the ingredient that had enabled her husband and herself to successfully negotiate life together—through good and ill, through joy and sorrow. Dietrich Bonhoeffer has suggested, "It is not your love that sustains marriage, but from now on it is your marriage that will sustain your love."[16] Marriage enables love to deepen and become creative along every avenue of interpersonal development. God constituted marriage to be a school of love; he meant marriage to facilitate the growth and maturing of love in its broadest and deepest dimensions.

Learning Mature Love

Have we, in the maturing and mellowing-out of love, banished all possibility of idealization? Are we now so realistic and reasoned in our loves that all traces of romanticism have been forever removed? Can we credit the sophistication of our day with separating love from romanticism? If so, then love has been stripped of its lyric quality and reduced to something less than what love was intended to be. To calm and stabilize emotions and passions is one thing; to do away with them is quite another. To come to terms with overidealizations is necessary, to be sure; to eliminate all idealization is, on the other hand, to quench something equally necessary to the human spirit and critically so to love. Love and romanticism do not fall into a neat either-or.

Love more mellowed-out will, of course, realistically check idealizations against what the loved one might reasonably become. But it retains the vision of possibilities for growth, delighting to see the beloved in his or her most favorable light. And why not? Love is most congenial with faith and hope. In that greatest of love's interpretations, I Corinthians 13, the three are conjoined—love, hope, and faith. Love can do no other than to hold high the vision of what might be. Love is also warmly emotional and communicates on an emotional level as well as on a physical, intellectual, and practical level. Love is social yet it remains uniquely personal. One's beloved is regarded as incomparably special, worthy to be one's sole object of desire. He loves her, and she loves him, because in the eyes of each the other is God's chosen one, and hence the very best of all possible choices. So peak experiences, never-to-be-forgotten moments, shared pleasures, romantic surprises are all to be expected along the way. Dull indeed would be the love in which there were no spontaneous moments of new discovery, new joy, new dimensions of pleasure. The beautiful thing is that there is a lasting quality inherent in this developing love, because it is founded solidly upon the commitment to caring. Faith, hope, and love!

What is so bad about a married pair concentrating on one another's more attractive qualities and minimizing the less appealing features? The wise always find little ways to make life more pleasant by accentuating the positive. Because it is never perfection that we seek, neither is it perfect realism or perfectly dispassionate reason that we expect in the finest marriage. After all, we are not machines. So couples need not strain to achieve some form of perfectionism, nor need they prove anything to anyone other than to themselves. Their basic motivation should be toward continual growth, not perfection now. So it is here that a little idealization may play a splendid role; it may even prompt a self-fulfilling prophecy. As one partner entertains an ideal of the other, the other may respond by seeking to become what his or her mate envisions; that is, if the ideal is not altogether out of range.

How many spouses could witness to the actuality of this growth in response to a healthy expectation and encouragement? It is axiomatic that a partner who truly loves becomes a growth facilitator in the life of the other. This is the creative nature of love at its best.

Perhaps I should say just a word about the relation of love to freedom. Individual identity is not submerged by the union that is marriage; at least it is not intended that this happen. Love and freedom go together; in fact, freedom is a precondition for love to grow. This is a glorious paradox! In contrast with romantic love—which is bondage—mature love is a magnificent release to be one's self. Love enables two people to grow in their sense of "we," but not at the expense of their sense of "I." So love is both binding and releasing at the same time—thus the paradox. Two people become one in that mysterious fusing of personalities, but never at the loss of a growing individuality. Primarily what love achieves is the mutual expression of acceptance and trust, allowing each mate the freedom to grow in a climate of confidence and support.

I've long forgotten who suggested the truism that love is a dialogue in which one person speaks and the other answers. In such a dialogue roles shift from one to the other in a rhythm of harmonious interaction. To understand one another, both must speak the same language. And what is that language, the language of love? Sometimes it's the language of emotion, sometimes of intellect, sometimes of the body. But in the profoundest terms of all it is spirit speaking to spirit. Love at its highest is a communion of spirits.

Erich Fromm has a profound word on love as communication: "Love is possible only if two persons communicate with each other from the center of their existence-
. . . . Love, experienced thus, is a constant challenge; it is not a resting place, but a moving, growing, working together."[17] And for Christian marrieds, as we shall see in the next chapter, if Jesus Christ resides at the center of their existences, the spirits of two will be as one. In the truest sense they will be one in the Spirit of God.

We began this chapter with a specific theme: Love is something we learn. Our deepest need is to be loved, our greatest work to give love. It seems equally true that to do the work of giving love is one way to fulfill the need to be loved, for love has a strange way of returning to the giver! In closing we return to the theme with which we began, letting a sensitive spirit speak the final word. In *Letter to a Young Poet*, Rainer Maria Rilke writes:

> For one human spirit to love another: that is perhaps the most difficult of all our tasks, the ultimate, the last test and proof, the work for which all other work is but preparation. For this reason young people, who are beginners in everything, cannot yet know love; they have to learn it. With their whole being, with all their forces, gathered close about their lonely, timid, upward-beating heart, they must learn to love.[18]

One haunting question remains: What if a person has not learned love? What if one has learned nonlove instead? Is such a one doomed to a nonloving life span of

years? Does this early learning render a person unmar-
riageable? Or worse yet, to be unhappy and unfulfilled in
marriage? Is one banished from love forever, blackmailed
by early, unasked-for learning?

The chapters ahead contain a positive, resounding *no* to
these questions. Love can be born in the breast of a redeemed person, quickened by the power of the indwelling Christ of God. We are made new creatures Christ, and
basic to our spiritual renewal is the experience of God's
love in Christ and the love that is created in our hearts by
the Holy Spirit.

~ 6

All Loves Excelling

> True love's the gift which God has given,
> to man alone beneath the heaven;
> It is the secret sympathy,
> The silver link, the silken tie,
> which heart to heart, and mind to mind,
> In body and in soul can bind.
>
> SIR WALTER SCOTT, *Lay of the Last Minstrel*

*W*E TURN to the New Testament for an extraordinary revelation of the nature of love—the love of God expressed in the life, ministry, and redeeming death of Jesus Christ, God's son, our redeemer. Here and here alone we discover a truly meaningful model for Christian married love.

God Is Love

A Christian assumption is that if God is the author and creator of all things, he is the author of love, the highest and noblest of all personal virtues the human mind can conceive. The New Testament doesn't disappoint our expectation. Not only is the fact of the transcendent love of God declared unequivocally, but there we have disclosed the incredible enactment of this love in the person of his Son. No example of love known to man surpasses that recorded of Jesus; this has long been the deepest conviction of minds of all the ages. Jesus' love is incomparable. And in the final analysis, all Christian theology may be said to be a theology of love. Creation, redemption, the glorious eternal fulfillment—all are the work of divine love. In Scripture we are taught the source of love, its nature, its action, its consequences, and its glory.

The apostle John gives us a brief but systematic and highly significant theology of love, going back to the very love nature of God, then describing love's enactment in Christ, and finally pointing to its application to Christian believers. John's Gospel is the Gospel of God's love, but it is in his First Epistle that the theology of love more fully finds expression. There we find the premise underlying everything else John has to say; it is simply this: "God is love" (I John 4:16). That all authentic human love is derived from God is expressed in 4:7, "Love is of God, and he who loves is born of God and knows God." Just how closely human love is related to God's active presence in the Christian's life is brought out in verse 12: "If we love one another, God abides in us and his love is perfected in us." In verse 16 the basic premise is repeated once again, "God is love," and the derived nature of human love is also repeated: "He who abides in love abides in God." Thus it is the authentic Christian, the one who truly knows God and has experienced the redeeming love of Christ, who can go on to a higher understanding of that love, the love that transcends anything known by those outside of Christ. And how does it work? What is the effective mechanism? We will come back to this in detail, but suffice it here to hear John declare, "We love because he first loved us" (4:19).

As a statement of John's basic premise, "God is love," I have found none finer than that of Dietrich Bonhoeffer:

> God Himself is love. Only he who knows God knows what love is; it is not the other way around; it is not that we first of all by nature know what love is and therefore know also what God is. No one knows God unless God reveals Himself to him. And so no one knows what love is except in the self-revelation of God. And the revelation in Jesus Christ, God's revelation of His love, precedes all our love towards Him. Love has its origin not in us but in God. . . . "Herein is love, not that we loved God, but that he loved us, and sent his Son to be the propitiation for our sins" (I John 4:10). Only in Jesus Christ do we know what love is, namely, in His deed for us. . . . The New Testament answers the question "What is love?" quite unambiguously by pointing solely and entirely to Jesus Christ. He is the only definition of love. . . . Love is always the revelation of God in Jesus Christ.[1]

This is the sum and substance of everything this book would make clear: *Love is knowing Jesus and the power of his loving!*

Learning from the Greek New Testament

The Greek in which the New Testament was written has three words translated in English by our one word *love—eros, philia,* and *agape. Eros,* from which we get *eroticism* in English, is not found in the New Testament at all. This is interesting inasmuch as *eros* is the word that most pointedly would be used for romantic love as we've described it. Quite simply, the New Testament is not at all concerned to address itself to romantic love. The other two words, *philia* and *agape,* are both found in the New Testament, *agape* being the more prominent. The distinctions brought out by all three words are still useful, all three describing qualities properly found in a healthy Christian marriage. Each makes its own special contribution to marriage.

Eros—Passionate Love

Eros is passionate love that desires the other for oneself. *Eros* seeks in others the fulfillment of its own hungers. It is any form of longing, seeking love that expresses desire for basically self-satisfying rather than altruistic reasons. It is selective and discriminating, seeking out the particular love object that holds promise of satisfying its needs. *Eros* is thus dependent upon the other person's ability to meet its expectations.

Before we are too hard on *eros,* we must see it as originally a created good, an appointed form of human love that was subsequently distorted and corrupted by human sin. *Eros* stands in need of redemption. The good news of the Christian faith is that *eros* is redeemable! The Christian need not banish *eros* to utter darkness; within the comprehensive scope of Christian love *eros* has its rightful place.

Because we are all individuals having unique qualities and capabilities, there is provided in the very nature of things a basis for making personal choices. That we desire to select and to be selected by a particular person on the basis of individuality is perfectly good and proper. To be special to another person because of what we are in ourselves reflects two significant things: the glory of the creative diversity expressed in individuals, and the glory of the human capacity to perceive those differences and to choose from among the many. Thus in its uncorrupted state *eros* is a useful means of selecting and relating to a mate. And though sometimes *eros* may be little more than romantic desire, it can be more than that; it can be desire for the whole person as a valued being. What is good about *eros* is that it does discriminate worthfulness. Choice grounded in individual worth is a very proper part of the creative order that finds its fulfillment in love's choice of a marital partner. But this is only part of it.

Eros becomes less than love whenever it separates itself from its created purpose. *Eros* becomes altogether self-oriented in the context of human sinfulness, and when this is the case, it seeks another only as a means of fulfilling its own selfish gratification.

Eros begins as little more than response to some external attraction, be it beauty, sex appeal, personal charm, warm friendliness—some special feature that makes a particular person seem unique. Because so often this has to do with something sexual, we've come almost automatically to imply something with sexual overtones when we use the word *erotic*. By definition, then, *eros* is desire motivated by some value outside of the lover. In sinful reality *eros* is largely a form of self-love, incapable of loving another for what that other is. As Reinhold Niebuhr has observed, *eros* "is always arrested by reason of the fact that it seeks to relate love to life from the standpoint of the self and for the sake of the self's own happiness."[2] The loved object, in the final analysis, is not an end but a means to an end

("It" rather than "Thou"). Unless *eros* is redeemed, it remains inherently tragic, predisposed to ultimate failure every time.

Because *eros* always expects something in return, it is utilitarian. But this is an unstable state at best. *Eros* in and of itself fosters the very opposite of committed, caring, responsible love. No wonder *eros* is subject to early disappointment and final disillusionment; by itself, *eros* is capable of turning love into hostility and resentment with frightening speed.

The fatal fault with *eros* unredeemed—as with romantic love—is that, because it hinges on its valuing of the love object, that value must remain constant if *eros* is to continue the same. So here again we face the law of diminishing returns, for the values *eros* seeks cannot forever remain what they are at the start. Time and familiarity erode the perceived value once so urgently desired. *Eros* has a rightful place, to be sure, but it must be a redeemed *eros*, integrated with *philia* and *agape*, and through their action controlled and informed.

Philia—Friendship Love

Philia speaks to the natural attraction between members of an intimate group, such as family or friends. It speaks of natural affection and attachment. Much broader than *eros*, *philia* is solicitous love, love that accepts the whole person as he is, liking him for himself not just for some part of him. The Greeks used it generally to designate a love that stood above passion and selfish possession, thus differentiating it from *eros*. It is based on reciprocity between parties. Sometimes *philia* indicates the quality of *liking* compared to the more intensive quality of *loving*. Once, in John 16:27, *philia* is used of God's love for humanity, and once, in John 5:20, it is used of the father's love for the son—a unique usage, as elsewhere *agapao* is the verb consistently employed. Paul used the word *philia* only twice. But even the limited use serves to accentuate the friendship dimension of complete love. This, as we are seeing, has its place in a full, balanced love between spouses. As the three Greek words overlap in meaning and use, so the qualities of love that each describes belong to a full-orbed marital love. Each, then, contributes to the completeness of love in human experience.

Agape—Caring Love

The verb *agapao* often translates as "to show love," because it is love giving, love active on another's behalf. It is always used to denote the love of Jesus for his disciples, the love of the disciples for one another, and especially the love of Jesus for the Father.

Conjugal love, like every authentic love, must be placed at the service of something transcendent—something outside the lover—for only in this way can love resist the attrition of time and habit. The noun *agape*, as it is used in the New Testament, in most cases describes a love with this transcendent quality. Of course, we must recognize that it's not the Greek word *agape* that tells us anything about the love of God; rather, it is the description of God's love that invests the word with radical new meanings and with far greater dimensions than were comprehended before. Perhaps no other Greek term owes so much to early Christianity. And although we search far and wide, only in God does *agape* exist as an absolute quality; in human beings it remains entirely derived.

Agape is not born of a lover's need, nor does it have its source in the love object. *Agape* doesn't exist in order to get what it wants but empties itself to give what the other needs. Its motives rise wholly from within its own nature. *Agape* lives in order to die to self for the blessedness of caring for another, spending itself for the sake of the beloved. Thus *agape* is not conditional love, that is, love conditioned upon an expected gain in return. It is not an act of self-gratification by means of another. Rather, its desire is directed outward from itself so as to be wholly other-centered. Thus *agape* stands almost in opposition to *eros*. But this would be too extreme a distinction; it is better to say that the dominant thrust of the two look toward different ends. Canon Charles Quick clarifies, "Whereas in *eros* desire is the cause of love, in *agape* love is the cause of desire."[3] Agape is neither evoked nor affected by some special value perceived in the love object. *Agape* is nothing less than God's ideal—altruistic love. As such it could only exist in God himself. Our concern, beyond understanding this ideal, is to ask how it may be appropriated so that in a very real way it may infuse, enrich, and control our *eros* and *philia*. In other words, how may God's *agape* redeem and transform our human loves?

God So Loved the World

When the New Testament says, "God so loved the world," just how great is "so loved"? The answer comes in God's mighty act of redemption: "God so loved the world that he gave his only Son" (John 3:16). Here is incredible, incomparable self-giving—no less than the self-sacrifice of God in the person of his Son! And for whom? For sinful, God-rejecting human creatures! The creator spending himself in order to redeem the creature: This is the measure of divine love, love without limit!

Certain implications of God's incomparable *agape* have been drawn by theologians in every age. Human beings were made in the image of God, yet that image was marred and people disabled by sin. In consequence, they were alienated from God in every respect. Nonetheless, God loved people still, not because they were lovely or lovable but solely because they needed love and God by nature is *agape*. God loved people simply because it is his, God's, essential nature to do so. God needs no further motivation than his own *agape*.

By all the scriptural evidence, God was not moved to give himself in redemptive sacrifice by anything he might receive in return. Not that he didn't know and rejoice in the anticipation that multitudes would come as a result to share with him in an eternal communion of love. But his act was not initiated with that in mind; it was a wholly unconditional act, motivated by love alone.

Such love is above being earned or deserved by humanity, nor could it be paid back in any way. Love so freely given is neither increased by whatever goodness humanity may possess nor decreased by whatever sinfulness it may manifest. It is not in any way affected by human goodness or badness, merit or demerit. Nevertheless, because humanity is in fact sinful, *agape* necessarily comes as mercy and as grace. As theologian Emil Brunner put it some years ago, in contrast with *eros*, which loves "because of," *agape* loves "in spite of." That is grace. As grace, *agape* is given freely upon God's own initiative. As mercy, *agape* is given to the undeserving, indeed, to those deserving the very opposite. So, to the undeserving (mercy) *agape* is given freely (grace). Biblical scholar C.H. Dodd said of *agape* that "it is not primarily an emotion or affection; it is primarily an active determination of the will. That is why it can be commanded, as feelings cannot."[4] The same notion is stressed by Martin Buber: "One cannot command that one *feel* love for a person, but only that one deal lovingly with him."[5]

Unconditional *agape* is love that can be trusted. Contrary to what we learned as children—that love is conditional and unreliable—God's *agape* is not subject to change; it is reliable. It remains unchanging in the face of every kind of disappointment. Robert Browning's word is recalled: "Love does not alter when it alteration finds." Nor is *agape* vulnerable to external forces that might oppose it. This is why Paul could ask, "Who shall separate us from the love of Christ?" and in reply range throughout the universe, only to say that nothing can separate us, nothing at all!

God's *agape* comes to us with creative purpose and power. Its very first effect is to awaken in the receiver the desire to live by and reciprocate a like love. It also empowers redeemed men and women to love one another with *agape*. The miracle is that God's *agape* creates its own response in the human heart. The key Scripture bearing upon this dynamic is I John 4:19: "We love because he first loved us." Despite our incapacity to love as we ought, we receive the power to love as we open ourselves to God's incoming *agape*. Thus we find that *agape* is the mightiest, most radically life changing of all creative forces within the sphere of personal relationships.

First *agape* draws us back to God from our alienation and hateful indifference. Then it infuses us with a new love for God and subsequently for others as well. As redeemed men and women, we are drawn into the communion of self-transcending, divinely originating love. We learn how self-transcending *agape* applies to each of our relationships. From this radical new perspective Christian couples can view marriage as that single relationship most perfectly suited to expressing the divine quality of love.

The apostle Paul explains the mechanism of how *agape* may be infused into our hearts; it is "because God has given us the Holy Spirit to fill our hearts with his love" (Rom. 5:5 TLB). In Galatians 5:22 Paul tells us that the fruit of the Spirit is, first and foremost, love. So by means of the Holy Spirit *agape* is received as a gift of God to our spirit, given for the purpose of transforming our human love inside of marriage and outside of it as well.

Agape transfigures everything it touches. As two partners share Christ's love, they find their love developing in unexpected ways. No marriage can be the same; couples are completely reoriented in all their incentives for living. It is exciting to see the love of Christ finding a particularly glorious expression within such a relationship as marriage.

Supremely, in Christian marriage, ruled by *agape*, one is loved for his or her own sake, for his or her worth in God's sight. Yet even beyond that Christian love focuses not on the other person as such but on the other person in relationship to Christ and his purpose. In the fullness of such love Christian spouses can say, "I love you for who you are in yourself, for who you are in Christ, and for who you are as God's special gift to me. I can also love you for the appointed place you share in God's purpose for our life together."

As Rollo May observes in *Love and Will*, love represents a number of affectional systems found within a single relationship, the incorporation and integration of which is a major task for personal development. Like other perceptive students of love, May sees the three—*eros, philia,* and *agape*—integrated together. Although *agape* is the highest, purest form of love, it does not replace or supersede either *eros* or *philia*. Rather, those two forms are enriched and controlled by *agape*; it is *agape* that permeates them both. Or, as Sherwin Bailey expresses it in *The Mystery of Love and Marriage*, the relation between Christian lovers is that of natural love restored and transformed in Christ, enhanced by the addition of a new quality—*agape*.

Agape as Creative Forgiveness

Open to all who share *agape* is the magnificent new possibility of experiencing creative forgiveness. What is meant by creative forgiveness? What makes this central to the success of Christian marriage?

Uniting two autonomous human beings in marriage is fraught with the ever-imminent danger of incompatibility, disagreement, and conflict—all divisive forces. Our self-protective mechanisms cause us to take adversary positions even with those we love the most. We are quick to defend our opinions and tastes, to promote our preferences, and at times to manipulate our mates to get something we want. Miscommunication leads to misunderstanding and to personal hurts, real or imagined. In every possible way we are opened wide to conflict, just where it can escalate most easily.

It is never long after the wedding is over before a couple has the first occasion for a jarring disagreement, perhaps an argument, something that seems shattering to the "shining shield" romantic love had wrapped around them. One partner is hurt and the other blamed as the offending party. It may have been just thoughtlessness, but it hurt. How do we deal with this? There is an urgent need for the offending mate to acknowledge offense and for the offended party to accept an apology in a forgiving way. But will it happen this way?

The problem of achieving forgiveness is that two egos stand in the way. Pride is unwilling to bend in the direction of forgiveness. Why, we think, shouldn't the offense be punished properly? And why shouldn't justice be administered? Is one supposed to just take it? So goes our thinking. Nonloving thoughts begin to take over, justified by the fact that, however great or small or how nondeliberate the offense, it represents a letdown of love.

But marriage is a love relationship all the way, and at the very heart of *agape* is redemptive grace, abundant mercy, and a forgiveness that regards the partner's welfare and growth as more important than any pleasure gained in meting out justice. If Jesus taught us anything, it is nonretaliation and unconditional forgiveness as the way of love. We are to forgive others in the same manner in which God forgives us. Is this not Paul's word in Ephesians 4:32: "Be kind to one another, tenderhearted, forgiving one another, as God in Christ forgave you"? As married couples, we are to model the forgiving love of God in Christ.

Forgiveness is not, as Swiss psychiatrist Paul Tournier pointed out, *being lenient*, that is, tolerant of the offense. This would constitute a denial of the offense and its serious consequences, minimizing the offense, putting it off as lightly as possible. One offended partner may say, "Oh, it's OK—no big deal! Sure, I was hurt, but let's forget it. I'd rather not make something out of it."

But being lenient is not what either party wishes. The one who has committed the offense wants to confess it, to make an open acknowledgment, desiring the other's forgiveness in return. Leniency precludes the opportunity for forgiveness. The better way is the scriptural way: "Therefore confess your sins to one another and pray for one another, that you may be healed" (James 5:16).

The gift of forgiveness cannot be less than mercy and grace. Nor is healing anything other than a spiritual process involving willingness on the part of both spouses to be humbled before one another and before the Lord. He knows the faults and failures of both. He gives grace to surmount the prideful defensiveness we naturally bring to such instances. For one partner to give and the other to receive this God-like gift of forgiveness requires their surrender to the Lord. Nothing short of this will ever suffice. I am talking about far more than the simple negotiation of two people's differences with an agreement to be reconciled. This is part of it, to be sure, but forgiveness stands far above negotiating a difference; it is facing the fact of hurt and healing it with the special touch of *agape*.

We can see at once that the demands of forgiving love cannot possibly be met with any ego-strength we might muster for the occasion. Forgiving love is something quite beyond the power of our desire let alone our will. Only incoming *agape* is adequate for this. It takes the Savior living in our hearts and controlling our spirits to enable us to forgive and to receive forgiveness.

So, quite simply, forgiveness is not a soft attitude toward a harsh reality, nor is it merely an act of appeasement in order to keep peace, in order not to make a bad situation worse. Nor is it being lenient or tolerant. Forgiveness is the full action of creative *agape*. Redemptive realism looks beyond the hurt to the possibilities of suffering transformed into good. Thus forgiveness is *mercy*—forgiving when there is no reason for doing so. It is also *grace*—taking the initiative to heal the broken relationship freely and without any demands guaranteed. Nothing is held over the head of the forgiven partner as though stored for future reference just in case there is a repeat of the offense. Forgiving love holds no reservations. Neither is it ever an act of condescension, calculated to elevate one's own esteem by lowering the esteem of the forgiven partner. Instead, creative forgiveness seeks to establish an even deeper basis for mutual respect and equality between the two partners. The only love capable of this is *agape*.

How beautiful is forgiving love—a mighty force for creating good out of ill! It goes hand in hand with other Christian virtues, such as humility, compassion, tenderheartedness, patience, all so essential to the full maintenance of love.

Integrating Eros and Agape

It is human to seek what we need—*eros*—but divine to seek what another needs—*agape*. This is true, but it's not the whole truth. A danger is that we make such a separation of the two loves as to think that married love should be only *agape*. In fact, *eros* and *agape* are meant to be integrated into one all-encompassing love.

Bishop Anders Nygren, in his famous work *Agape and Eros* placed the two loves in absolute, irreconcilable opposition to each other.[6] In actual experience, however, the two types are not that distinct. The Catholic scholar Martin C. D'Arcy is more realistic, saying that a love in which the self did not enter would be no love at all. "It becomes nonsense," D'Arcy writes, "to rule out all reference to self. To rule out the self is to make an abstraction of love which has no reality."[7] With this Sherwin Bailey concurs: "In every act and movement of the spirit by which lovers reach out toward one another, *eros, philia,* and *agape* are indistinguishably mingled."[8] And theologian Paul Tillich said that *eros* is commonly understood to be the desire for self-fulfillment by the other, whereas *agape* is the will to self-surrender for the sake of the other. But this alternative, Tillich explained, does not exist. The so-called "types of love" are actually "qualities of love," lying within each other, driven into conflict with one another only in their distorted, or absolutized forms. No love, said Tillich, is real without a unity of *eros* and *agape*.[9]

Tillich's view prevails today, leading contemporary theologians such as Lewis Smedes to call for a balance between *eros* and *agape*. Smedes points out our need to be loved because of what we are *(eros)*, yet also and equally loved in spite of what we are *(agape)*. We need to know that a loved one is special first of all, desired above all others and chosen because of his or her uniqueness. *Agape* complements *eros* by incorporating the whole person as the object of desire, and doing so for other than selfish reasons. *Agape* makes the other person the object of reverence as well as of desire, transcending but not disregarding all that *eros* finds attractive. Says Smedes, "*Agape* can manage the fact that *eros* will not find perfect fulfillment; *agape* is realistic but not judgmental, not given to disillusionment or despair." *Agape*, gratefully, has restorative powers even when *eros* seems to have died. Smedes goes on, "Since *agape* reverences the essential person, not some attractive aspects of that person, it can transcend the losses of time, and can create loveliness just through its persistence in loving."[10]

Smedes shows that *eros* by itself can easily turn to exploitation. First, it begins as need. Need arises out of desire, then progresses to demand, later moving to manipulation. The true counterbalance is *agape*, the love that is able to prevent this ultimately unfulfilling progression.

Far from standing opposed to *eros*, then, *agape* redeems *eros*, mitigating its selfish preoccupation and infusing it with a whole new dimension. Thus *agape* stabilizes, corrects, and enriches *eros*. No longer is *eros* isolated as a purely self-seeking love but is integrated with *agape* to form a balanced, full-orbed love, a love in which desire continues to have its proper place alongside the altruistic, self-giving qualities of *agape*.

One of the dangers of *eros* is that it always threatens to cut itself off from *agape*; left to itself this is the direction it takes every time. But when *agape* is there to turn it around, then the two forms of love can function together within the larger dimensions of marriage. It is always *eros* that needs direction and control, always *agape* that can supply it.

Larry Christenson has a balanced position on this in *The Christian Couple.* He suggests that if husbands and wives were to seek to love one another so purely, asking nothing in return of each other, it might deteriorate into a patronizing form of love, cold and distant and hardly human. He writes, "The Bible is at once more profound and more practical. It sees a husband's love for his wife springing not from disinterested altruism, but from a profound personal unity."[11]

Part of the instability of *eros* is that it knows intuitively that the beloved, for all his or her attractive features, cannot be all that *eros* wants. *Agape* knows this too, but does not regard this imperfect fulfillment to be a contradiction of love. Instead, *agape* sees all manner of disabilities, deficiencies, and imperfect fulfillments as a deeper call to love, as demanding no less than one's entire and willing commitment to the beloved.

Whereas *eros* tends to die in the achievement of its own ends, *agape* can never die, for it doesn't depend for its life upon self-fulfillments, transient and uncertain as these are. *Agape* happily gives itself to the limitless possibilities of being the caring, ministering servant. *Agape* is servant love.

Now that we've seen the superior nature of *agape*, it is only natural to want it for ourselves in fullest measure. We must say, however, that in no human relationship is the ideal of *agape* ever fully achieved. In fact, nothing in Scripture suggests that it is perfectly realizable aside from the one earthly example—the life of our Lord Jesus Christ. Nevertheless, *agape* remains the perfect ideal to be approximated as fully as possible in the power of the indwelling Spirit of God. We do aim for it!

Special Command to Husbands

Now we are prepared to understand what Scripture means when it addresses the great command to husbands, "Husbands, love your wives as Christ loved the church and gave himself up for her" (Ephesians 5:25). The whole mystery of creative and reciprocal love is embodied in this command. It is the logical counterpart within marriage to the love-relation between Christ and the believer. Love creates its own response. In loving his wife, the husband elicits her returning love. The receiver becomes then a giver; love is born of love. Not that this is the whole of it, of course, but it is the critical element, the added dimension so essential to the ultimate success of married love.

No loftier ideal could God have put before husbands. The fullness of Christ's love for the church suggests five major characteristics for husbands to emulate by the power of his indwelling Holy Spirit. Years ago I outlined these in the book *Design For Christian Marriage,* and I will summarize them briefly here.

(1) *Christ loved the church realistically.* He was under no illusions, romantic or otherwise, when he sought us in love. Nor was his love sentimental. John doesn't say, "For God so felt a sentiment of emotion toward us that he gave his only Son. . . ." No; he knew us just as we were—sinful, prideful, unloving. Our only capacity for love was to direct it toward ourselves. God, by contrast, was motivated solely by his caring love for us. He willed to restore the lost image and the broken fellowship through redemption. Our desperate need only induced deeper dimensions of self-giving to his love. How realistic was he!

No two people can afford to be so realistic with each

other as can redeemed men and women, those who seek to pattern their married love after the model given them by Jesus. Their love can afford to embrace every fault and failure, every unlovely and disagreeable thing. Jesus' love internalized and shared is adequate to this demand, so husbands and wives can follow his example—loving realistically rather than romantically.

(2) *Christ loved the church sacrificially.* He "gave himself up for her." How costly is love! I John 3:16 reads, "By this we know love, that he laid down his life for us." That is, he first counted the cost then paid it willingly and joyfully. So here we have the model of self-sacrifice. *Agape* takes a husband outside of himself; his happiness is found in paying whatever cost is required to secure his wife's happiness and well-being. This is his chief aim in being a husband.

(3) *Christ loved the church purposefully.* His purpose is expressed in Ephesians 5:27, "that he might present the church to himself in splendor . . . holy and without blemish." Whose splendor—his? No, hers! His purpose is the eventual perfection of his bride. The Christian husband can love his wife with a similar purpose in view—love determined to encourage whatever will bring about the development and realization of her potential. And the all-embracing goal? That she might become all that God intends her to be. Could any wife hope for greater love than this?

(4) *Christ loved the church willfully.* *Agape* is not only, or even primarily, an affair of attraction or emotion. Love is *intentionality*—determined love. Although I did not comment on it earlier, in both the Septuagint version—the Greek rendering of the Old Testament made prior to

Christ's time—and in Paul's letters *agape* stands for God's electing, covenant love. This is accented by Paul's frequent use of the term *agapetos*—the chosen one. The idea comes from as far back as the Old Testament prophet Hosea, in whose writing love is viewed as faithful, covenant love sustained with God's chosen ones. All these ideas—electing, faithful, covenant love—transfer over to the New Testament concept of married love. In this cluster of concepts we have a mighty essence.

More than anything else, love is *commitment*. This takes love out of the area of emotion altogether and makes it an activity for the whole personality—mind, heart, and will—all cooperating in the act of loving. Amid all the contemporary forces that tend to separate couples and send them on their individual ways, it is the commitment of love—loving willfully—that is of highest importance to the creation of enduring marriages. How badly we need to recover this dimension of commitment in our time!

(5) *Finally, Christ loved the church absolutely.* His love is without limit, without condition, and without reserve. Ephesians 5:28 reads, "Even so husbands should love their wives as their own bodies. He who loves his wife loves himself." Unlike the first standard of love's measurement—Christ's love for the church—this is a human measurement. Although less than a divine standard, it is a good and useful one nonetheless. For it says simply that a husband would no more neglect his wife's well-being than he would neglect his own body. Love, according to this standard, supplies all that is needed in nurture, care, and protection. For a detailed list of love's highest attributes, a couple should read together I Corinthians 13, acknowledging to one another the degree to which they are

prepared to commit themselves to each specific aspect of love. And to make this reading even more a personal, spiritual discipline, a couple could do no better than also read together the fine book by Lewis Smedes, *Love Within Limits*.[12]

The degree to which Christian married love must become a commitment to caring is the theme of the next two chapters. We need to take love out of the abstract and set it down in the day-to-day lives of husbands and wives. That is, we need at long last to utilize our new, more complete understanding of love in a concrete way. What one word shall we choose to sum up the essence and activity of *agape?* The word is *caring.* As we make the transition to the theme of caring, a fine thought from Larry Christenson serves to prepare us:

A genuine, caring love is like a tree that is mature. It does not get uprooted by every passing wind of feeling or change. It develops with time a strong root structure. It sends out sturdy branches. It can survive dry spells. It can product healthy fruit. It is in every sense a healthy tree. Feelings do not direct such love, only enhance it.[13]

～ 7

Commit Yourself
to Caring

When the satisfaction or the security of another
person becomes as significant to one as one's own
satisfaction or security, then the state of love exists.

HARRY STACK SULLIVAN, *Conceptions of Modern Psychiatry*

*I*N THE course of examining love in its many different modes, we've moved steadily forward toward the New Testament ideal—*agape* love, an active, giving love that is placed in the service of another person. It is not born of need in the lover except as there is need to give oneself for the welfare of another. It is not motivated by an expectation of self-gain; *agape* love is other-centered. Found perfectly in God, this love may be internalized within the Christian man or woman who allows the Spirit of God to do his work.[1] Some may say, "Well and good, but can you go a bit further and put a handle on this love? Can you narrow it down to a certain action? How can I know that I am truly loving?"

Love as Caring

At the heart of every truly successful marriage there is a husband and wife, intimately teamed together, who above all else have learned to give each other the gift of a caring self. The central passion of their devotion to each other is to be caring partners, caring in everything that touches their life together. Whatever else a couple may wish to give each other but for some reason cannot, they can—if they will—give the very highest gift of all: *a caring self.* At its finest and best—and incidentally, its most rewarding—love is essentially a process of reciprocal caring.

Other forms of love exist in their own right; we've seen this to be so. But which love is most fundamental, most encompassing, most worthy of the name? It is caring love. To describe a couple's successful togetherness as *love* is not specific enough; in fact it is quite meaningless. But to describe it as *caring* is to invest the general idea of love with tangible and useful meaning. Caring is the term that puts a handle on love. It gets beneath the romantic idealizations and ego-trips, beneath the sexual aspects, to the real gift so satisfying to give and so satisfying to receive.

If, as we've seen, we tend to romanticize love, sometimes to mystic heights, it cannot be so with caring. We cannot remain in the clouds and at the same time take full note of real needs and give ourselves to meet those needs. In other words, romantic love does not make room for caring, and caring removes one from the illusions of romance. Caring brings us down to earth again. Inasmuch as caring calls for tangible evidence of its presence, it is far less easy to glamorize in any respect. The rather amazing thing is that we can convince ourselves at times that we love our wife or husband even when we are not very caring in terms of giving ourselves to the other. Seen in this light, caring is the true test of love. Whatever we think is taking place, the real question is this: Am I manifesting caring love?

Is caring more attitude or action? This is not the right question, for caring is both. Perhaps more frequently the attitude or feeling comes first and then is translated into action. We feel and desire, then act out those feelings and desires. But we know that caring may develop in just the opposite fashion. When one deliberately sets out to care for another, to give oneself in an act of caring, it is amazing how often the feeling of deep care follows. More than we suspect, caring is a matter of the will.

Interestingly, in one of the few passages in the Bible where the word *caring* is found, both attitude and action seem to go together: "Casting all your care upon him; for he careth for you" (I Peter 5:7, KJ). It is interesting to observe in the King James version how human burdens and needs are described as "cares." We care for those who have cares.

God didn't simply sit in the heavens above and shout down through a cosmic megaphone, "I care for you!" No; he acted out that caring love, saying it best in what he did. In the coming of Jesus to give himself on Calvary for our sins we have the highest model of a caring God. This is not the only evidence of God's care for us, but it certainly is the highest.

From creation we also learn of God's special care; he created us in his own image, in every respect dignifying us by forming us for an intimate relationship with himself. He lavished his care upon us in his abundant provision for our every need. There was nothing that we could desire that God hadn't provided. And when we sinned against him, God was the one most deeply hurt. Yet although we were estranged from him, God cared enough not to condemn us, not to execute judgment upon us. Instead, he made possible a gracious gift of salvation, a gift given at incredible cost to himself. He cared enough to love the unlovable, unconditionally. In fitting response we sing, "No one ever cared for me like Jesus."

God's Caring and Our Caring

Recall once more our earlier discussion of the principle laid down in I John 4:19: "We love, because He first loved us" (NASB). Here is our model, but, more than that, here is the source of our own capability to love.

Christians have the blessed privilege of knowing that they are cared for by their father above; that they are loved, accepted, forgiven, empowered to new life and love. They know that they live within the gracious providence of a caring Lord. They learn what it is to live out that care through their own lives in the world, constantly encouraged and enabled to do so by their Lord. Thus within them is built a foundation for becoming caring people. Their feelings of self-worth are established in the knowledge of their infinite worth to the Savior. They can love because they are loved, care because they are cared for. Whatever their earlier experiences of nonloving, whatever patterns of nonloving have become habituated, Christians are given a whole new foundation upon which to stand. They are subject to the renewing power of their caring God who leads them out into a like caring.

As in every age, Christians today are called to live out his love, reenacting his care in the world. As Christ gave his life for the church, so the church gives its life for the world—by caring first of all. The church has irresistible power when it is a caring church. And notice how readily this fact disposes of the question of whether the church is socially involved in the world or only involved to the extent of proclaiming the Gospel. A caring church is involved in the lives of those it seeks to reach with the Gospel; it offers the cup of cold water in the name of Jesus!

By the same inner dynamics marriage has irresistible attraction when it is a caring relationship. Whenever two Christians are brought together in marriage, the stage is set for their mutual growth as caring partners. Committed to a permanent, exclusive relationship, they have every supporting condition to develop a caring partnership.

Caring and Personal Development

Is a person's capacity to love related to how much he or she was loved as a child? Psychological studies shed an interesting light on the relation between caring and human development. It has been shown that, depending on the degree of maternal deprivation, infants will die because no one cares sufficiently for them to live, they will survive as helpless creatures who are unable to deal with reality, or they will enter into adult life emotionally crippled. It is frightening to contemplate the damage to human life that results from a deprivation of caring love.

Says child psychologist Willard Gaylin in his book *Caring*, "Since the human being requires some eighteen to twenty months of fetalization, of which only nine months can be spent within the womb, an alternative supportive and nourishing mechanism is required. The caring attention of the mother is the substitute for her womb—the persona of the mother replaces her placenta."[2] Summing up the evidence, Gaylin says that for any full development into personhood, with the capacities to communicate and relate, it is necessary for the child to be loved in a caring way. Being loved in this way initiates in the child the capacity to give love to others. "The degree to which we are nurtured and cared for will inevitably determine the degree to which we will be capable of nurturing and caring."[3] So it becomes abundantly clear that each of us is the product of those who have cared for us or have refused to care for us.

What individuals bring to marriage reflects the degree to which caring was a part of their early experience. Many individuals bring into marriage an array of emotional needs, including the scars of early care deprivation, but if they are fortunate to have a spouse who is committed to caring, this can be the means of reversing the accumulation of negative attitudes and behavior. If there is a deficient sense of self-worth at the root of an irritable personality, the caring spouse can make the partnership the place where extraordinary growth can happen.

Caring is the magic key that unlocks the gate into an intriguing world of marital contentment. For those young people who are presently measuring romantic love against what they perceive married love to be, let us just say that contentment far surpasses excitement as the reward of love. Before entering the gate of caring into the world of marital contentment, however, we see a prominent warning that the way ahead is largely unfamiliar. Even mature, experienced adults will have to learn how to travel this way. We are cautioned that there may be some hard decisions to make. Formidable obstacles will be encountered; of that we can be absolutely certain. The way is not only difficult but costly as well. Some failures are inevitable. But the warning also emphasizes that exceptional satisfactions await all married pairs who are willing to explore the rich and expansive terrain in this land of caring. None will be sorry to have gone this way; it is more than worth the cost.

To be a caring person is to be a growth-facilitator; it is to commit one's time, thought, and energy to helping another person grow and become fulfilled or self-actualized. Contemporary philosopher Milton Mayeroff clarifies this facet of caring in his statement "Caring is the opposite of simply using the other person to satisfy one's own need."[4]

If there is any one flaw that especially disables marriage, it is the tendency to use other people for one's own ends. This behavior can be so subtle at times as to go unrecognized. We try to make other people the means to our own satisfactions. Although we may reward them for serving such purposes, we are using them nonetheless, and this is to violate the integrity of their personal self. A greater evil appears when we regard ourselves as entitled to the services of others. Using people is the opposite of loving them.

Whether it be for one's child, a friend, or a spouse, caring is treating another as having full and equal personhood. Any less regard violates the personal integrity God has appointed, diminishing the other person to the status of a thing to be used for one's own selfish purposes. How often, for example, do uncaring husbands or wives claim ownership rights, acting as though they were entitled to do as they pleased with their mates. But all of that changes when a passion for caring becomes central to the relationship. A caring mate reorders all the values and priorities of married life in the direction of the spouse's fulfillment.

The Power of Caring to Change People

We've noted how early and continued rejection, or the withholding of self-affirmation, can deprive the child—later the adult—of rightful feelings of self-worth. Conversely, giving care can be the creative force in establishing a person's identity as a valued individual, worthy of love and trust. Caring has the power to change people. Whenever we can look at ourselves and say, "See, someone cares for me! I'm valued for who I am!" we are motivated to desire further growth. Furthermore, we seek to justify the care and trust we have received. Now we are free to accept ourselves, to care for ourselves, to live with greater self-confidence, and to become caring people ourselves.

As Mayeroff puts it, caring inspires us to have the courage to be. Negative feelings toward ourselves and toward our world are turned, as if by magic, to positive feelings. We feel better about ourselves, and, as a result, every aspect of our personal development follows more positively. We grasp the possibility of becoming more than we are because of the new hope born within. We begin to see ourselves as capable of caring, too. At this point we can say that caring has come full circle; it has created in another individual its own response. Herein lies the miracle of caring.

It is fascinating how, with caring, one's awareness undergoes a radical change—not so much in the big things as in the little things. It so often seems to be the little matters that most easily irritate self-centered, ingrown people. Yet an accumulation of small irritations can begin to alienate the best of partners; or if not alienate, keep life from being its brightest and best. I can present an example or two from my own life.

In our home we would rarely have a fire, despite the fact that there is a fireplace in the living room and another in the family room, because I dislike building fires. I have never enjoyed cleaning ashes, getting up into the soot to turn the draft regulator, assembling kindling to start the fire, and then keeping it going. But the other side is that my wife likes a fire in the fireplace; it is one of the simple pleasures that she enjoys a great deal. The whole issue suddenly becomes this: Do I care enough for her and for bringing pleasure to her to want to have fires in the fireplace? My pleasure lies in sharing her pleasure, and this is sufficient pleasure to overcome the displeasure of building fires. It is a test of caring. I could put my arm around my wife in the evening and whisper "I love you, dear"; but if I still do not feel motivated to build a fire, I am not caring.

Another rather insignificant matter concerns the division of labor in our home. We've been married for thirty-five years and have always had a tacit understanding as to who does what in our home. We've never quarreled about this, and it has only seemed natural that my wife does certain things and I do other things. With the advent of dishwashers it seemed appropriate that she load and unload the dishwasher. Of course, I soon forgot that the dishwasher meant that I never shared the task of drying dishes. And so it has gone for quite a number of years. It only recently dawned on me that I could do this at least occasionally and relieve a bit of drudgery. I learned immediately that a stack of stoneware dinner-size plates are heavy. But I also learned that I have pleasure whenever I do this—not the kind of pleasure that is merely slapping my own back, but that of knowing I did something to please my wife.

For some couples it could be the need to improve their communication. Sharing life verbally, listening and questioning so as to actively participate in each other's day, is a meaningful way to affirm one another. Sometimes it is a matter of sharing time more generously. The use of leisure time is a measurement of caring.

Perhaps it is learning to share the cultural enjoyments of the other even though it means learning a whole new area of interest. One partner's profession or work may occupy first place to the point of obscuring the caring role almost completely. Or worse, the call to Christian ministries in the church may take a husband or wife away for an inordinate amount of time. Responsibilities for the children, the home, church, or school activities may lead to neglect of one's role as caring mate. One is reminded of the motto, *Beware the barrenness of a busy life.* Busyness may at times be a subtle substitute for a caring role at home. The barrenness is further reflected in noncaring ways. It is all too easy to get caught up in perfectly good activities, only to lose sight of our more important role as caring spouse.

To specify in just what ways a married partner is not caring may be difficult, yet it is not difficult to feel when this is the case. Nothing can generate conflict more quickly. If there is no central passion for caring, our values and priorities simply will not find their proper balance. On the other hand, when there is a disagreement, mates who are habituated to treating each other in caring ways will find the resolution to their conflict comes more easily.

There is a basis of trust that caring has generated, and that stands a couple in good stead when the going gets tough.

Like most growing things, caring grows slowly. Only with time and experience does it mature and blossom. It requires the deepening of the relationship through the long accumulation of days counted as years. This is why nothing can compare with the beauty of a relationship in its later years, when it is marked by the ripened growth of caring. But caring must begin early if the relationship is to deepen at all.

Caring always moves outward in concentric circles from the center of one's most intimate life, never inward. Like ripples in a pool when a rock is dropped into the water, so caring starts with those closest to us, then moves out to touch others. Where the associations are most intimate and the responsibilities most personally demanding, there caring finds its point of origin. It cannot be otherwise. Individuals who cannot care for those closest to them, yet suppose themselves to be very caring to those outside that circle, are under an illusion. The husband who prides himself on being a caring employer but who is a neglectful person, insensitive to his own wife and children, is not caring at all. He is winning brownie points in the office, impressing others for his own ego's sake.

Caring and Maturity

Paradoxically, it takes maturity to be a caring person, yet it is in being a caring person that one matures; the two qualities are inseparably linked together. But each of us must begin somewhere, and that somewhere is in trusting

God to grant us the capacity to start caring and then to grow within the process. No one can perfectly meet the conditions for being a caring individual. The most mature will only approximate those conditions. Caring individuals, congruent with their objectives, give trust, ask for trust, and in turn show that they trust God for their own growth and capacity to care. So we can say that mature people are growing in their active life of caring. Caring takes on deeper and broader dimensions when it is the action of a mature person. Similarly, a caring person cannot help but become more mature as a consequence of caring.

To become that caring partner in your marriage, you must be able to give positive answers to a series of questions. As a concluding exercise designed to take the central message of this book—*agape* love expressed as caring—and make it as personal and practical as possible, we shall consider a group of such questions. But first let's take a final look at the nature of caring, reinforcing some of the major ideas that have come before us.

Mayeroff has written to demonstrate that the highest claims of love are represented in the call to care for one another. There is no higher claim of love, no higher evidence of the love of Christ; this is the essence, the very life of love. Recall once again our brief notice of I Peter 5:7: "Casting all your care upon him, for he cares for you" (KJ). Translating that to Christian marriage, can a wife say, "I can cast all my daily cares upon my husband, for he cares for me"? Or can a husband say, "I can cast all my cares of this day upon my wife, for she surely cares for me." No husband or wife with a balanced, mature insight is going to want to dump all his or her cares upon the other; an inordinate dependency can be created in this way.

And, too, there is such a thing as overburdening a spouse who is not prepared to carry such loads. There must be wisdom in this, and we would not imply otherwise. The point, however, is that caring is a growing capacity in genuine love to carry one another's burdens, and this is scriptural (See Gal. 6:2). A Christian couple will also put into effect the promise of Psalm 55:22: "Cast your burden on the Lord, and he will sustain you" (KJ).

Perhaps the most significant thing we can say of anyone is that he or she is a caring person. This is the quality people look for most, the quality that most inspires trust in another. This is what fortunate children possess in good parents, and really what lovers seek in each other.

We noted earlier that caring changes people. What people? Not only the individuals cared for, but those who do the caring. For instance, it is little less than amazing what happens to people who are morbidly introspective. With life turned completely inward, such people are tightly bound to their own burdens. Life is distorted because they cannot see beyond themselves. What can better lift such people above the compounded burden of self-absorption than to direct thought and energy alike in a caring concern for someone else? Thus it is that caring is a standing challenge to a self-centered existence. For caring is totally incompatible with ego-building and status seeking. Caring turns inward-looking people into outward-looking people, contributing to the change of perspective for one thing, behavior for another. And inevitably it is change for the good.

Rollo May said, "Care is a state in which something does matter. . . . The good life comes from what we care about."[5] Or, as we might say, *"who* we care about." And

May is not alone in his assessment. Philosopher Martin Heidegger earlier had written that caring is the basic phenomenon of human existence, that which constitutes man as man.[6] For Heidegger, when we do not care, we lose our very being. Care also, in Heidegger's concept, is the source of conscience. "Conscience is the call of Care," and "manifests itself as Care."[7] This is a sweeping concept of humanity, centering our essence in our capacity to put mind, affections, and will into the service of caring. Likewise, the world-famous cellist Pablo Casals, interviewed just before his death, when he was in his nineties, summed up life in these words: "I feel the capacity to care is the thing which gives life its deepest significance."[8] And Erich Fromm states: "If I love, I am in a constant state of active concern with the loved person."[9] *Concern* here stands for *caring.* So we see how leading observers of human relationships agree that caring is the essence of loving.

When one person says to another, "I love you," the beloved has every right to know what the other really means. Is it, "You're the one I want to commit myself to, to give myself to so that whatever comes I shall intentionally care for you and for your highest welfare"? Anything less than such caring intention is mere sentiment and not love.

One thing we might learn as married people is that the problems we face in an uncaring spouse may relate more to his or her early experience of life with uncaring parents. This keeps the condition from being blameworthy. Gaylin quotes the psychiatrist H. Lichtenstein: "Caring is the process by which the mother gives birth to the individual her infant will become."[10] In other words, each of us represents in our personality the imprint of a mother's care. When we meet uncaring attitudes and behavior in a spouse, we must seek to understand the cause, then go about finding ways to correct it. The beautiful thing to give hope to hurting spouses is that caring can change an uncaring person into a caring one.

One final thought on the nature of caring before we move on to a practical consideration of how this is to work in marriage. Bob and Margaret Blood in their college text *Marriage* expand the concept of caring as follows: "Beyond caring responsiveness to the needs of the other, lies confirmation of the other as a person. ... When I confirm your right to be different from me, I look forward to your accepting my differentness from you. If our relationship is to be healthy, each of us must be an authentic person. In confirming your otherness, I appreciate the vitality and the energy with which you take charge of your life and make it into what you feel led to become. ... Confirmation at best becomes gratitude for the other's existence. ... This is the point at which love transcends mere coziness and becomes mature."[11] Caring is more than acceptance; it is full confirmation of the partner's being and becoming.

~ 8

Building a
Caring Lifestyle

To live without loving is not really to live.
MOLIÈRE, *La Princesse d'Elide*

*T*HIS chapter presents ten questions designed to help you take inventory of your present status as a caring person, especially as a caring partner in marriage. You may wish to return to these questions later on, keeping them as a checklist to determine just where you are and what you are becoming as a loving, caring person. Very possibly there is no person for whom these questions will not be painful to some degree, for they aim at a high standard. If this is the case with you, don't give up. With God's help you can grow step by step into the model he has given. You can experience the miracle of caring, Christian love.

1. *Have I sufficient sense of self-worth that I can look away from myself and see my mate as a deeply valued person worthy of my utmost caring?*

Before you can have positive feelings about any other, you must have positive feelings about yourself. We speak of this as positive self-regard, or positive self-worth. We all tend to project our own self-feelings, positive or negative, onto others. Self-acceptance and self-love are prerequisites to the caring life. Where do you see yourself in this regard?

For us as Christians the issue of self-acceptance should be settled when we know that we are fully accepted by God on the basis of the redemption we have in Christ. We have been loved with an everlasting love, accepted in the Savior's own righteousness. God has given us infinite value as his redeemed child. What God has loved, we can now love. What God has accepted, we can now accept. What God has valued, we can now value!

The problem may be your partner's low self-esteem. Your spouse may respond to your caring from the disadvantaged position of a poor self-image, perhaps even saying, "I'm not worthy of your love and care." What does unrequited caring do to you? Do you tend to become frustrated, to pull back, and to think to yourself, "Well, if that's all he (she) thinks of my caring, why put myself out for that?" But this is an ego-response, the opposite of a caring heart. You must see that the problem is your spouse's low self-valuation—a problem that has its only chance of a solution, perhaps, in your caring.

You must seek to be strong in the Lord and in your own sensitivity, seeing your worth in Christ and not in the eyes of your partner. Otherwise you will become defensive and distant, no longer able to care. You must be able to meet indifference, slight, or even overt hostility. Despite the vulnerability you feel, you must seek to open yourself to your loved one and assimilate all such responses into a caring spirit. It is here as nowhere else that you need to experience the caring power of God.

2. *Do I care enough to dedicate myself to my partner's growth toward reaching full potential as a person in his or her own right?*

You must be sure that your desire to care for your spouse is not something you choose to do because you feel constrained to act out some sentimental idealism. This motivation would never last. Nor would you be able to meet the hard demands nor find the strength to care consistently. Even less appropriate would be choosing a caring role because of a need within yourself to have the satisfactions which such a role might bring. Rather, you must be committed to your loved one as a person whom you greatly value. You must be committed to his or her growth, whatever that requires of you. This will bring a constant reminder that your loved one has intrinsic value beyond any specific value to you. Your partner is more than an extension of yourself; indeed, is an individual with value in his or her own right.

This being the case, you should seek to establish and maintain an equality between the two of you. For apart from any assessment of your mate in human terms is the infinite value God has given. This means that caring will always see the person not the performer.

Thus we may view caring as a sacred trust: You are ultimately accountable to God for the way you care for your spouse. Here we are talking about a task with greater than human requirements. Are we not also talking about the greater than human resources at our disposal? So from the perspective of God, who cares more than you can possibly care yet who enables you for the task, you can see the potential for your beloved's growth—growth within your care. But it all depends on your own relationship with the Lord who wants to set you free to grow and to be a growth facilitator too.

In the process of being a growth facilitator, it is important not to create a dependency in your loved one—an interdependency, yes; a dependency, no. Caring liberates; it does not control or dominate or manipulate. You are called to liberate your beloved, so he or she may be more open to self, to life itself, and to be more in touch with self and others. Will you not ask God for the strength to make such a commitment?

3. *Am I willing to order all my values and activities around caring, making it the primary aim of my marriage and all else secondary?*

Mayeroff comments: "Caring has a way of ordering activities and values around itself; it becomes primary and other activities and values come to be secondary."[1] Many things previously felt to be important will now fade in significance, and things related to caring will take on a new importance. What is found to be incompatible with caring, you must exclude; what is found to be irrelevant to caring, you must subordinate. In other words, you are to safeguard the conditions that make caring possible.

This is no easy task. It doesn't happen automatically. Rather, it requires conscious and continuous surveillance over all that touches your life. The more precious a relationship, the more it warrants safeguarding. So it is by the safeguards you employ to protect it and the sacrifices you make to sustain it that you show the worth of the relationship in your own value system. Caring partners will realistically count the cost and commit themselves to pay it.

Does all this sound as if intolerable restrictions are being assumed? Is it the same as giving up one's personal freedoms? To the inward-turning person this most surely will seem the case. But do not all our freedoms have built-in restrictions? Do we not give up one freedom in order to gain another? Do we not lay aside one set of plans or one set of values in favor of another? In other words, do we not choose one freedom over another?

In the commitment of marriage I recognize that I am no longer free to maximize my opportunities for pleasure and comfort if I am to maximize my ministry of caring for my loved one and thus to have the deeper satisfactions that caring brings. So, depending upon the goals that you set for your marriage, you will relinquish certain freedoms in favor of the more important commitments.

Caring provides that all-important center around which your values, activities, and life aims may be integrated. And this reorienting around a new center brings harmony to your life as a whole. It diminishes the potential for living a fragmented existence, beckoned in many directions and diverted by lesser objectives. Even the contradictions of your life are lessened. Caring draws you away from the more peripheral claims, which you will more readily recognize as of secondary importance. It is not too much to say that caring liberates us to a new simplicity of living.

With such abundant satisfactions awaiting you, will you not accept God's invitation to become a caring spouse? Will you not seek to let caring order all your values and activities around itself, so that it may become the ruling principle, with all else subservient to it?

4. *Am I willing to accept the new demands and new disciplines that caring may impose upon me?*

Caring is not only giving something but taking on something—new demands, new disciplines. This is unavoidably a part of the nature of caring. In which of two possible ways will you respond to these demands? Either they are evils to be endured or creative opportunities to be grasped. Caring is meant to be the catalyst that transforms what you are obligated to do for your mate to what you are delighted to do. Yet, even in those instances where duty does not become delight, caring partners can accept the demands and disciplines because caring has its own rewards and satisfactions.

You ask, *But what do I do when it's hard to care?* This is a common and understandable question. We might let James 1:2–6 shed some light on the personal benefits to be gained from the tests and trials that God allows:

> When all kinds of trials and temptations crowd into your lives, my brothers, don't resent them as intruders, but welcome them as friends! Realize that they come to test your faith and to produce in you the quality of endurance. But let the process go on until that endurance is fully developed, and you will find you have become men of mature character with the right sort of independence. (JBP)

Though caring brings with it new demands and disciplines, this does not amount to a new bondage. Quite the opposite! Caring liberates us, removes from us the restrictive bondage of self, opening us up to the significance of giving ourselves willingly to our loved ones. All of life opens out.

Notice the shift in emphasis; we are talking not only about the gift of caring but about the discipline of caring. What happens when caring becomes the central meaning of one's life is that life as a whole is brought under discipline. This translates into the discipline of time, interest, labor, leisure—every area of life. Quite clearly, caring is the only passion that can motivate one to such an encompassing discipline of life. Are you prepared for this? Do you see your marriage in this light?

5. *Am I willing to pay the ultimate price of caring: to make continual acts of self-relinquishment as caring shall require?*

Because the sole aim of caring is the welfare of a loved one, caring shifts the center of life from self to other. Self-relinquishment becomes an act of will, not emotions. It is deliberate and reasoned, decisive and continuous. If you are willing to pay this price, be prepared that everything within you will combine to throw up a line of resistance. And the task will not be made easier by your living in a culture that stresses self-fulfillment as the aim of all living. In such a social climate, self-relinquishment may seem too high a price to pay to be a caring partner.

There is, of course, legitimate and necessary self-interest within a caring relationship. It is only when our self-interest stands in the way of caring that it loses its legitimacy. Here lies the inevitability of conflict in a relationship as intimate as marriage. You must be prepared to accept the fact that caring not only imposes new demands and disciplines, but it also creates some new conflicts as well.

Our caring thus will be put to a severe test at times—
the test of our maturity to resolve conflict in a caring way.
Can you enter into another's point of view when it is not
your own? Can you make appropriate compromises when
it seems necessary to harmonize two lives? Can you post-
pone what otherwise might be an impulsive response? It
is in the crucible of conflict and its resolution that your
highest self can rise, purged and refined in the process.
For it is in losing yourself for the sake of another that you
find yourself. If this is true in a general sense, it is especially true in a marriage.

6. *Am I willing to care enough to be an open and fully self-
   disclosing mate, even though it means being vulnerable and
   unprotected?*

It is humbling enough to know oneself, but even more
humbling to be known by another—truly known by a
significant other. Yet self-disclosure is a decisive element
in caring. The self-disclosure of one person helps open another to being a self-disclosing person as well.

To disclose oneself means to acknowledge failures and
offenses, apathy, indifference, and even one's utter insen-
sitivity at times. For inevitably there will be breakdowns
in caring, selfish retreats from facing up to the demands
and disciplines. Along with these will come the negative
attitudes such as lovelessness and resentment. How de-
pressing and self-defeating are lapses such as these! But
when they are humbly faced before God and made subject
to his forgiving grace, one is set free once again, able to
amend the fault and to move on to caring once more.
How skilled is our God in turning failures into new be-

ginnings. His grace transcends failure and utilizes it for good.

No caring partner has a greater desire than to assure his or her mate, "You can count on me; I won't ever let you down. I care too much to fail you." Nevertheless, it is human to fail. Beyond confession to God that brings the assurance of his forgiving grace, there is the place of confession to a loved one. James 5:16 reads, "Therefore confess your sins to one another, and pray for one another, that you may be healed." Confession of a sin or offense against your mate is a special reaching out in love, giving opportunity to your spouse to respond in a significant way. It is an opportunity to respond with forgiveness and acceptance. The lapse in caring invites your loved one to care for you in a very needed way.

Are you willing to be a self-disclosing partner, fully known and with nothing to conceal? Are you willing to give up a life of little secrets? Will you risk what this kind of vulnerability may mean? Can you forgive or receive forgiveness as the occasion requires? Are you willing to take the lower place in order to exercise caring? If you can do this, you can be caring and at the same time not condescending, failing at times yet not defeated.

Is it ever right to confront the person you care for? Yes. Risk taking sometimes means caring enough to confront. This is the theme of a splendid book by theologian David Augsberger entitled *Caring Enough to Confront.*[2] Think of those times when the one you love has taken a wrong or harmful direction. Though you may be committed to helping his or her growth without imposing your own values and aims unduly, nevertheless there are times when this ideal is not altogether possible. Then your ultimate allegiance is to the truth as you understand it in God's word. In instances where not to intervene would seem a compromise of God's will, you must care enough to confront. It becomes your responsibility to step in gently and understandingly, seeking in love to alter the other's course. In Ephesians 4:15 Paul refers to our "speaking the truth in love"—how basic this is for both caring and communication.

It is true that this is not always the decision you will come to. Risk taking under the guidance of God's Spirit sometimes means taking the option not to confront, not to intervene at all. If your caring holds good promise of bringing about a reversal of the wrong course without the necessity of confrontation, this may well be faith's proper decision. Just to stand by and suffer for the present may be God's answer, for he alone sees the end from the beginning. It is precisely at such times that caring partners will rest their trust completely in the God who leads because he cares.

7. *Is my caring so controlled by the Spirit of God as to also incorporate faith and hope?*

Faith, hope, and love are mentioned together in I Corinthians 13 as having a close interrelation. Though love is said to be the greatest of these three, it does not appear to stand apart from the other two. Interestingly, it is in caring that we see the coming together of all three.

Where does faith fit in with caring? Caring is a test of faith. As Christians we must first accept by faith that caring is part of God's will for our lives, especially within our marriages. It takes faith to believe that God will work through our limited capacity to care, accomplishing his purposes for the growth of our partner. Further, it takes faith to believe that God will direct and empower our caring, enabling us to be sensitive, empathic, and patient. Caring means having faith in whatever outcome God chooses, assured that it will be a worthy outcome despite any seeming evidence to the contrary.

Faith also involves our willingness to commit ourselves to a largely unforeseeable future. Unlike ourselves, God sees the future as clearly as the present. The future is ordered within his providential care. And his purposes never fail! We must have faith that God is in the caring process and that he will perform his will, so we can continue on even when there is no evidence that our caring is bearing fruit in our mate's life. We shall not require any guarantees as to the outcome. But should we tend to dominate the relationship, to control or manipulate it, this would be evidence that faith is faltering. For faith never seeks to force growth. Quite the contrary; the caring individual learns to combine faith and patience, happy to leave the results with God.

Hope is the bright side of faith, that which inspires faith to see God doing the very best whatever the circumstances. Hope inspires faith to hang on despite every discouragement and to rejoice that the best is yet to be. Faith and hope will enable us to see the growth process in our mate, and to commit ourselves to encourage that growth with all our power.

8. *Do I accept God's purpose that caring is the central meaning of my life, fulfilling the deepest reason for my existence?*

Jesus himself set the course with his words, "I came not to be ministered to, but to minister" (Matthew 20:28). In another context he said, "He that is greatest among you shall be the servant of all" (Luke 22:26). According to Philippians 2:7, he who took the form of a servant is now our model. Paul sums up what is to be the central purpose in our lives in Philippians 2:5; "Have this mind in you which was also in Christ Jesus."

For Christians the whole world becomes increasingly intelligible the more we realize the central role of caring in God's plan for human life. It is this that aligns our lives with his, putting us in parallel motion with him. And the best part of it is that caring is inexhaustible; there are no limits to its possibilities! Yes, caring is living out the central meaning of our existence as God appoints it.

For married partners caring means that each spouse is privileged to participate meaningfully in the growth of the other and to enjoy the long-term benefits. Caring has its best chance to blossom in the marriage relationship, where there is commitment to both intimacy and permanence. Within marriage caring can be both intensive and extensive to the limits of human possibility. This is a great discovery and a great challenge. When caring occurs within this most intimate union, it enjoys a degree of intensity not to be found elsewhere. Because it also occurs within the scope of a committed union over a long period of time, caring achieves its most extensive dimension as well. Marriage affords every condition for caring to develop and mature. It is not too much to say that marriage is that interpersonal relation in which we may experience caring at its fullest and best. Caring is the most intensive within the intimate bonds of marriage, the most extensive within the life-partnership of marriage.

9. *Will I encourage my mate to become responsive to his or her own need to be a caring person responsible for the meaning of his or her own life?*

Remember that the one you care for most is a person just like yourself, a person with a twofold need—to be loved and to love. Because it is a natural response to want to reciprocate care in some way, you must be sensitive to every attempt made by your mate to return care and you must give every opportunity for a successful return of caring.

Think for a moment what would occur if you were to be indifferent to such returns of caring love or to deny it in some way? This would be tantamount to your no longer caring at all. How easy to crush the budding new life of responsive care! As a caring spouse, you should aim ever to encourage your mate to be responsive to the need to reciprocate loving care. It is thus that we can help our partners become responsible for living out the meaning of their own lives.

10. *Am I willing to take the place of a learner in general, and a listener in particular, so as to strengthen the dialogue of caring between us?*

If you are to know the person you are caring for and how best to meet his or her needs, you must assume the place of a learner. Only as a serious learner can you perceive the potential for growth in your mate. Most important, you must learn to think as the other thinks, feel as the other feels. Empathy is to become an "insider" in the life of another, seeing his world as he sees it not as you see it or wish he could see it. You enter into his life, his world. Central to the development of empathy is the building of an adequate communication network. How often do couples who are inwardly distant from one another complain, "We do not communicate." Caring is communicating at every level of personal life.

Learning comes largely through listening to both the verbal and the nonverbal messages directed to us. Listening is a highly demanding involvement, quite opposite of merely hearing what another says. Hearing is a passive process, listening an active one. Listening calls for the complete participation of the listener in the communicative endeavor of another. It is to offer the gift of one's whole attention, one's whole presence. By your listening, you say to the other, "I am truly accessible to you. I accept you and think enough of you to want to know what you are thinking and feeling, what you are seeking to communicate to me." Almost magically, listening opens people to one another, for listening is the gentle art of helping others say the things they long to say and of affirming them in what they are saying. Listening changes people by giving them the warm feeling that someone cares enough to give themselves in their entirety. Listening always helps reduce any feelings of mistrust or hostility the other may struggle with.

A powerful adjunct to listening is the skill of giving feedback, gathering up a piece of conversation and reinterpreting it in your own words, inquiring if this is what the other is saying and meaning. Thereby you seek to uncover the meanings beneath the outer wrappings of words spoken. Feedback gives additional opportunity to the communicator to clarify or to correct, or in some way qualify what was said the first time. Feedback is part of the adaptive skill of the caring person. And where better to learn this skill than in the commitment of the marital partnership? If you seek to do this for the sake of your own relationship, you might just turn the person you care for into one who also listens deeply and who grows into a more caring partner.

The Power to Care

All that we are talking about cannot be achieved in the power of the self. It is the power of God by his indwelling Spirit. He has promised us this power; it is ours to be appropriated by faith. Are you ready to make that appropriation?

Strikingly, it is in Ephesians that Paul speaks of this power, and in the same context he indicates something of the nature of caring without ever once using the word. In 4:2 he speaks of "forbearing one another in love." In 4:32 he speaks of being "kind to one another, tenderhearted," and also refers to "forgiving one another." In 5:21 he instructs us to "be subject to one another." As for the power to care, he says in 5:18, "Be filled with the Spirit." Caring is God's work, and we must let him do that work through us.

Our caring may or may not be reciprocated. Our fond hope, quite naturally, is that our caring will create a like response. And often this is just what happens. But so much depends upon the development of the other, upon his or her ability to respond. What is important is that we not make the expectation of response a part of our reason for caring. It is reason enough just to care! The basic question you must face is simply, *How much do I care about caring?*

How do you rate yourself as a caring person? How does this demonstrate itself in your family? Among your friends? In the opportunities for service that God places before you? What do you see blocking your growth as a caring person, and how can those obstacles be removed? Where do you most need to grow as a caring person? What specific steps can you name as part of that growth?

If you are a married person, you have the finest built-in relationship possible for learning love as caring. If you are looking forward to marriage, you are in a position to test your caring at the level of your present relationship and to assess the one you're interested in by this measurement.

From the myths and muddles of romantic love to the more mature, caring nature of Christian *agape* love, is a major step. No one can take that step in a single leap. Maturity in any area of life takes time and gradual growth. It is as you understand the characteristics of each form of love, and the process involved in growing away from the less desirable to the more desirable, that you can begin to evaluate your experiences and learn from them. It is in this way that you can avoid the pitfalls and set your course for the most enduring, most realistic most satisfying love of all.

Source Notes

Chapter 1

1. Suzanne Lilar, *Aspects of Love in Western Society*. New York: McGraw-Hill, 1965, p. 101.
2. Robert Briffault, *The Mothers: A Study of the Origins of Sentiments and Institutions*, vol. III. New York: Macmillan, 1927, p. 430.
3. Morton Hunt, *The Natural History of Love*. New York: Alfred A. Knopf, 1959, pp. 76–81.
4. Gail P. Fullerton, *Survival in Marriage*. 2nd ed. Hinsdale, Ill.: Dryden Press, 1977.
5. Bernard I. Murstein, *Love, Sex, and Marriage Through the Ages*. New York: Springer, 1974, p. 148.
6. Murstein, p. 148.
7. A. J. Denomy, *The Heresy of Courtly Love*. New York: D.X. McMullen, 1947, p. 59.
8. Murstein, p. 163. Also see M. Rosenberg, *Eleanor of Aquitaine*. Boston: Houghton Mifflin, 1937.
9. Denis de Rougemont, *Love Declared*. New York: Pantheon Books, 1963, p. 30.
10. Hubert Benoit, *Many Faces of Love*. New York: Pantheon Books, 1955, p. 13.
11. Charles Williams, *The Figure of Beatrice: A Study in Dante*. London: Faber & Faber, 1943.
12. Williams' work is given brilliant commentary in lay theologian Mary McDermott Shideler's *The Theology of Romantic Love: A Study in the Writings of Charles Williams*. Grand Rapids, Mich.: Eerdmans, 1962.
13. Williams, *The Figure of Beatrice*, p. 7.

14. Shideler, p. 31.
15. Ibid., pp. 33–34.
16. Charles Williams, *Religion and Love in Dante* (pamphlet). London: Dacre Press, 1941.
17. Shideler, p. 35.
18. "The Index of the Body," *The Dublin Review*, vol. 211, no. 422, July 1942, pp. 13–20.
19. Charles Williams. *He Came Down from Heaven and the Forgiveness of Sins.* London: Faber & Faber, 1950, p. 68.
20. Williams, *The Figure of Beatrice*, p. 28.
21. Shideler, p. 39.
22. Benoit, pp. 40ff.
23. Ibid., p. 116.
24. H. G. Beigel, "Love: Courtly, Romantic, and Modern," *American Sociological Review*, 1951, 16, pp. 326–334.
25. *Romeo and Juliet*, act 2. sc. 2, line 143.
26. Murstein, p. 181.
27. L. Stone, *The Crisis of the Aristocracy (1558–1641).* London: Oxford University Press, 1965.
28. N. Epton, *Love and the English*, Cleveland: World, 1960, p. 94.
29. Murstein, p. 200.
30. Hunt, pp. 171–173.
31. Johann Wolfgang von Goethe, *The Sorrows of Young Werther.* Excerpted by I. Schneider, ed., in *The World of Love*. New York: Braziller, 1964.
32. Charles Frankel, *The Love of Anxiety.* New York: Harper & Row, 1965.
33. Theodor Reik, *Psychology of Sex Relations.* New York: Holt, Rinehart and Winston, 1945. See pp. 126–136. Quotations from Reik in this chapter are taken from this volume.
34. Denis de Rougemont, *Love in the Western World.* New York: Pantheon Books, 1956.

Chapter 2

1. Andre Maurois, *Seven Faces of Love.* New York: Didier, 1944.
2. D. Day, *The Evolution of Love.* New York, Dial, 1954, p. 261.
3. Jean Jacques Rousseau, *The Confessions.* London: William Glaisher, 1883. p. 160.
4. Ibid., p. 382.
5. Marie Henri Beyle (Stendhal), *On Love.* New York: Boni and Liveright, 1927.
6. J.A.T. Robinson, *Honest to God.* London: SCM Press, 1963. Quotations from Robinson are from this volume.
7. Joseph Fletcher, *Situation Ethics: The New Morality.* Philadelphia, Westminster Press, 1966. Quotations from Fletcher are from this volume.

8. Paul Tillich, *Systematic Theology*, vol. I. Chicago: University of Chicago Press, 1951, p. 152.
9. Frederick S. Carney, "Deciding on the Situation: What Is Required?" In Gene H. Outka and Paul Ramsey, *Norm and Context in Christian Ethics*. New York: Scribner's, 1968, p. 5.
10. Quoted in Maurois, p. 147.

Chapter 3

1. J. Viorst, "What Is This Thing Called Love?" *Redbook*, February 1975, p. 12.
2. See articles by Lawrence Casler and Rogers Wright in *Symposium on Love*, ed. Mary Ellen Curtin. New York: Behavioral Publications, 1973.
3. Raoul De Sales, "Love in America," *Atlantic Monthly*, May 1938, pp. 645–651.
4. William M. Kephart, *The Family, Society, and the Individual*. 3rd ed. Boston: Houghton Mifflin, 1972, p. 345.
5. Gail Sheehy, *Passages: Predictable Crises of Adult Life*. New York: Bantam Books, 1977, p. 96.
6. See "Love." In *The Philosophy of Santayana*, ed. Irwin Edman. New York: Random House, 1942, pp. 101–102.
7. Erich Fromm, *The Art of Loving*. New York: Harper & Row, 1956, pp. 4, 53.
8. See Herbert Otto, *Love Today*. New York: Dell, 1972, ch. 6.
9. Rollo May, "A Preface to Love." In *The World of Love*, ed. Isidor Schneider. New York: Braziller, 1969, p. 281.
10. Stanton Peele with Archie Brodsky, *Love and Addiction*. New York: New American Library, 1975.
11. Vernon W. Grant, *Falling in Love*. New York: Springer, 1976. Quotations from Grant are from this source.
12. William James, "Review of H. T. Finck, *Romantic Love and Personal Beauty*, *The Nation*, 45 (1887), pp. 237–238.
13. Goethe, *Faust*, I, 14, trans. Bayard Taylor. New York: Modern Library, 1950, p. 125.
14. Robert Grimm, *Love and Sexuality*, trans. David R. Mace. New York: Association Press, 1964, pp. 102–105.
15. Denis de Rougemont, *Love Declared*. Unless otherwise specified, quotations from Rougemont are from this source.

Chapter 4

1. José Ortega Y Gasset, *On Love*. Cleveland: World, 1957, p. 52.
2. Ibid.

3. Ibid., p. 69.
4. C.S. Lewis, *Christian Behavior*. New York: Macmillan, 1943, p. 32.
5. Benoit, pp. 7–11.
6. Quoted in Shideler, *The Theology of Romantic Love*.
7. Allan Fromme, *The Ability to Love*. New York: Farrar, Strauss, 1965, p. 252.
8. Aaron Rutledge, *Pre-Marital Counseling*. Cambridge, Mass.: Schenkman Publishing, 1966.
9. Lucy Freeman and Harold Greenwald, *Emotional Maturity in Love and Marriage*. New York: Harper, 1961, p. 8.
10. P. Géraldy, *"L'Amour."* In *The Compleat Lover*, ed. William Geoffrey. New York: Harrison-Hilton 1939, p. 7.
11. C.S. Lewis, *The Four Loves*. New York: Harcourt, Brace, 1960, pp. 18–20.
12. Robert Farrar Capon, *Bed and Board: Plain Talk About Marriage*. New York: Simon and Schuster, 1965, p. 81.
13. Sheehy, p. 125.

Chapter 5

1. Fromme, *The Ability to Love*.
2. David Jones, "Love and Life Goals." In *Love Today*, ed. Herbert A. Otto. New York: Dell, 1972, p. 228.
3. Walter Trobisch, *Love Is a Feeling to Be Learned*. Downers Grove, Ill.: Inter-Varsity, 1971, p. 9.
4. V.A. Demant, *An Exposition of Christian Sex Ethics*. London: Hodder & Stoughton, 1963, p. 74.
5. Rollo May, *Love and Will*. New York: Norton, 1969, p. 9.
6. Karl Barth, *Church Dogmatics*, III, 4. Edinburgh: T. & T. Clark, 1960, pp. 221–222.
7. John Macmurray, *Conditions of Freedom*. Toronto: Ryerson Press, 1949, p. 59.
8. Theodor Reik, *A Psychologist Looks at Love*. New York: Holt, Rinehart and Winston, 1972, p. 150.
9. C.S. Lewis, *The Four Loves*, p. 91.
10. See Ernest Havemann, *Men, Women, and Marriage*. Garden City, N.Y.: Doubleday, 1962, pp. 114–115.
11. See Derrick Sherwin Bailey, *The Mystery of Love and Marriage*. New York: Harper, 1952, pp. 30–33.
12. Nicholas Berdyaev, *The Destiny of Man*, trans. Natalie Duddington. 4th ed. London: George Bles, 1954, p. 200.
13. Peter A. Bertocci, *Sex, Love, and the Person*. New York: Sheed and Ward, 1967, p. 12.
14. Herbert A. Otto, ed., *Love Today*. New York: Dell, 1972, p. 244.

15. Fromm, *The Art of Loving*, p. 41.
16. Dietrich Bonhoeffer, "A Wedding Sermon from a Cell," *Letters from Prison*. London: SCM Press, 1967, p. 36.
17. Fromm, *The Art of Loving*, p. 103.
18. Rainer Maria Rilke, *Letters to a Young Poet*. Rev. ed., trans. M.D. Herter Norton. New York: Norton, 1954, pp. 53–54.

Chapter 6

1. Dietrich Bonhoeffer, *Ethics*. New York: Macmillan, 1955, p. 173.
2. Reinhold Niebuhr, *The Nature and Destiny of Man*. New York: Scribner's, 1949, p. 66.
3. Charles C. Quick, *The Doctrines of the Creed*. New York: Scribner's, 1938, p. 54.
4. C.H. Dodd, *Gospel and Law*. New York: Columbia University Press, 1951, p. 42.
5. Martin Buber, *Two Types of Faith*. New York: Macmillan, 1952, p. 69.
6. Anders Nygren, *Agape and Eros*, trans. Philip S. Watson. Philadelphia: Westminster Press, 1953.
7. M.C. D'Arcy, *The Mind and Heart of Love*. New York: Holt, 1947, pp. 69–70.
8. Bailey, p. 29.
9. Paul Tillich, *Dynamics of Faith*. New York: Harper, 1956, pp. 114–115.
10. Lewis B. Smedes, *Sex For Christians*. Grand Rapids, Mich.: Eerdmans, 1976. See pp. 92–98.
11. Larry Christenson and Norris Christenson, *The Christian Couple*. Minneapolis: Bethany Fellowship, 1977, p. 35.
12. Lewis B. Smedes, *Love Within Limits*. Grand Rapids, Mich.: Eerdmans, 1978.
13. Christenson and Christenson, p. 96.

Chapter 7

1. Material in Chapters 7 and 8 is adapted from *Marriage: Handle with Care* (a Regal Book), by Dwight Small. Copyright © 1977, Gospel Light Publications, Glendale, CA 91209. Used by permission.
2. Willard Gaylin, *Caring*. New York: Alfred A. Knopf, 1976, p. 78.
3. Ibid., p. 45.
4. Milton Mayeroff, *On Caring*. New York: Harper & Row, 1977, p. 1.
5. May, pp. 289–290.
6. Martin Heidegger, *Being and Time*, trans. John Macquarrie and Edward Robinson. New York: Harper & Row, 1962, p. 370.

7. Ibid., p. 319.
8. Albert F. Kahn, "The Meaning of Love," McCalls, vol. 97, no. 7 Pril 1970), pp. 70ff.
9. Fromm, *The Art of Loving.* p. 128.
10. Gaylin, p. 103.
11. Bob and Margaret Blood, *Marriage,* 3rd ed., New York: The Free Press, 1978, pp. 23-24.

Chapter 8

1. Mayeroff, p. 51.
2. David Augsburger, *Caring Enough to Confront.* Glendale, Calif.: Regal Books, 1973.